Making Silk Flowers

Making Silk Flowers

BERYL WASEY

B T Batsford Ltd, London

*To my late husband Victor, who gave me so much
encouragement in making these flowers over the years, and
to my son Richard and daughter Jill*

Illustrations by Jill S. Wasey

Photographs by Sue Atkinson

First published 1992
© Beryl Wasey, 1992

Typeset by Deltatype Ltd, Ellesmere Port, Cheshire
and printed in Singapore by
Kyodo Printing Co (Singapore) Pte Ltd

Published by
B. T. Batsford Ltd
4 Fitzhardinge Street
London W1H 0AH

A catalogue record for this book is available from
the British Library

ISBN 0 7134 6721 5

Contents

Part 2: The Flowers

Introduction

Flowers are so beautiful that it is only natural that we should want to fix them in some lasting form for pleasure and for comfort.

This book is designed exclusively for beginners and is intended to give a good grounding in all aspects of the art of flower-making. A variety of flowers can be made from silk and also from other fabrics – I have used plain old cotton sheets, pillow-cases and even old clothes with surprisingly successful results. You do not need any special skills; just an interest in nature, an eye for colour, and the ability to use a pair of scissors with moderate precision.

One point to remember before you begin is to keep in front of you, or clearly in your mind, an example of the flower you intend to make. Only then can you capture its true shape and colouring.

I am sure that, as you read this book and try making examples for yourself, you will appreciate how rewarding this pastime can be.

Beryl Wasey

Suppliers

U.K.

Khrmas Enterprises
87–89 Coronation Avenue
East Tilbury
Essex RM18 8SW
Tel: (0375) 843205
Fax: (0375) 857–266

Mrs B. Wasey
48 Grasmere Road
Chestfield
Whitstable
Kent CT5 3NA
Tel: (0227) 793099

U.S.A.

Mr E. Narsingh
95–01 103rd Street
Ozone Park
New York 11416
U.S.A.
Tel: (718) 847–9536/849–9253

The author's video on how to make silk flowers is also available from these suppliers.

Part 1

Equipment and Techniques

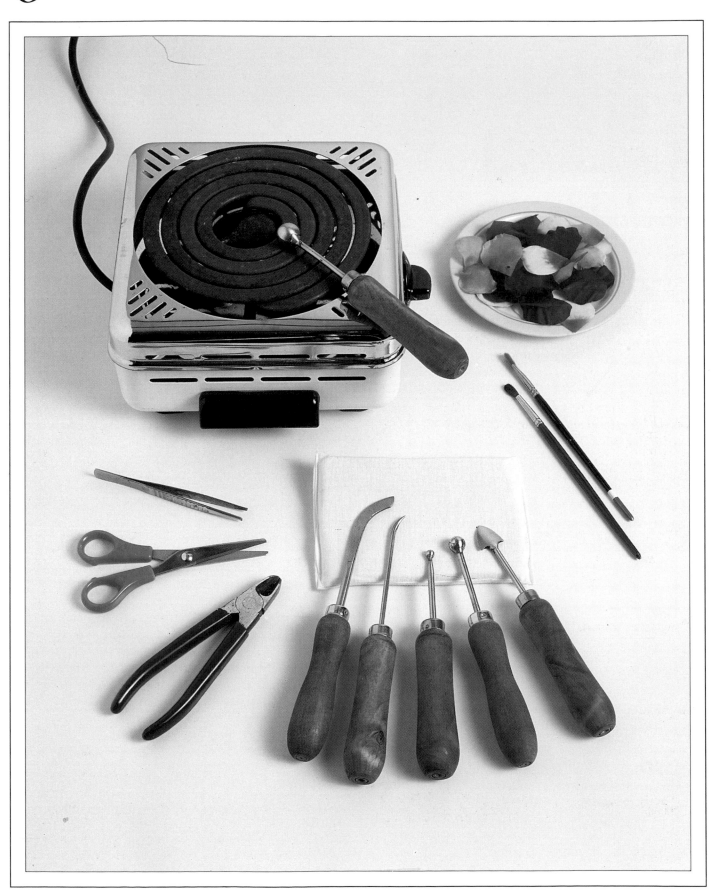

Silk flowers can be made using a few simple tools, listed here.

SCISSORS

A medium-sized, sharp pair is needed for cutting petals, leaves, etc. The blade is also used for curling paper stamens.

CUTTERS

Needed for cutting wires.

FOAM RUBBER

This acts as a mould for shaping petals, leaves, etc. Two thicknesses are needed: 13 mm ($\frac{1}{2}$ in) and 51 mm (2 in). Both types should measure 15 cm (6 in) × 10 cm (4 in) and be covered with cotton fabric. The 13mm ($\frac{1}{2}$ in) thickness is used mainly for marking veins and shallow hollows, as it allows the amount of pressure applied to be controlled. The 51 mm (2 in) thickness is used for creating deeper hollows. There is no reason why you cannot vary the

ball goffer ¼", ½", ¾"

chaser goffer 2-line

curler goffer

spade marker

Special tools for flower-making (available by mail order from the address on page 7)

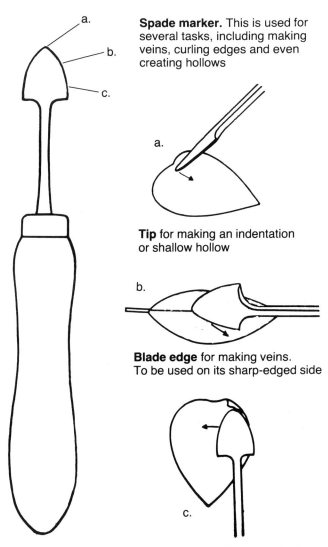

Spade marker. This is used for several tasks, including making veins, curling edges and even creating hollows

Tip for making an indentation or shallow hollow

Blade edge for making veins. To be used on its sharp-edged side

Blade edge for making curls on petal edges. To be used on its flat side

thicknesses used if you find that this makes it easier to shape the petals, etc. When making veins, you can also use a piece of cotton cloth, such as a tea towel, folded into four in place of the 13 mm ($\frac{1}{2}$ in) foam rubber.

SPADE MARKER

This extremely versatile tool, so named for obvious reasons, is used to create several effects. The edge is used for making veins in petals and leaves and for curling the edges of petals, and the tip is used for making hollows when heated. This tool should be used over the 13 mm ($\frac{1}{2}$ in) foam rubber for making veins, curled edges and shallow hollows.

CHASER GOFFER

This tool has a double edge, and so creates a double crease when heated, which is useful for flowers such as Carnations. It should be used over 13 mm ($\frac{1}{2}$ in) foam rubber.

BALL GOFFER

This tool is available in three sizes: 6 mm ($\frac{1}{4}$ in), 13 mm ($\frac{1}{2}$ in) and 19 mm ($\frac{3}{4}$ in). It is used to make hollows on flower petals when heated. The depth of the hollow varies according to the amount of pressure applied. By using 13 mm ($\frac{1}{2}$ in) foam rubber, a shallow hollow can be made, whilst a deep hollow is achieved by using 51 mm (2 in) foam rubber as a base. The 6 mm ($\frac{1}{4}$ in) ball goffer is used mainly on smaller flowers, such as Gypsophila (see page 61).

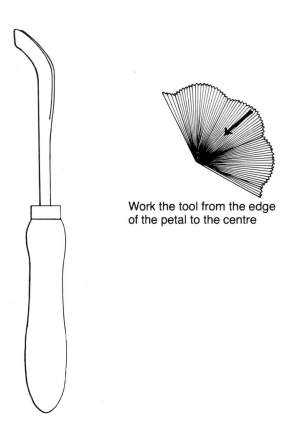

Work the tool from the edge of the petal to the centre

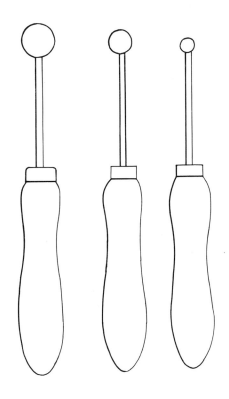

The **chaser goffer** makes creases on petals such as Carnations

The **ball goffer**, which comes in three sizes, is used to make curves and hollows on petals in calyxes. The depth of the hollow can be varied according to the amount of pressure applied

CURLER GOFFER

This is used to curl the edges of petals, and also makes a fluted edge when heated. It can also be used for piercing the centre of calyxes and sets of petals. This tool is used on both thicknesses of foam rubber.

PAINTBRUSH

A 51 mm (2 in) or 76 mm (3 in) paintbrush is used for applying starch to fabric. It should always be kept clean, so it is advisable to keep it for this purpose only. Rinse it thoroughly after use and allow it to dry before putting away.

ARTIST'S PAINTBRUSH

You will need two of these: an inexpensive, fine, round brush for tinting petals, and a medium, flat one for applying dyes and fabric paints to larger areas. These should also be rinsed thoroughly after use and allowed to dry before putting away.

TWEEZERS

These are useful for handling petals while dyeing and tinting. A long-handled pair with pointed ends is ideal.

PLATES AND DISHES

A flat plate is needed for laying the petals out while dyeing or tinting. Dishes are needed for mixing dyes and paints.

HEATING EQUIPMENT

An electric hot plate or gas ring (which must be covered so as not to burn the tool handles) is necessary to heat the metal part of the tools to the right temperature for flower making (see page 23).

CLOTH

Keep a piece of clean cloth or rag to wipe the tools before shaping each petal or leaf, particularly if the fabric is white.

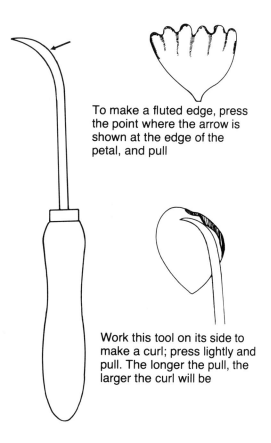

To make a fluted edge, press the point where the arrow is shown at the edge of the petal, and pull

Work this tool on its side to make a curl; press lightly and pull. The longer the pull, the larger the curl will be

The **curler goffer** is used for curled and fluted petal edges

13

Materials

The materials required for flower making, their uses and where to obtain them, are listed here. Certain fabrics are recommended, but there is no reason why you cannot experiment with others. It is advisable, when selecting your fabrics, to make sure you cannot see which way the vertical grain runs, and that the fabric has some elasticity. Knitted and nylon fabrics are not suitable. The only silk suitable for dyeing and tinting in flower-making is medium-weight habutai lining silk. It is available in off-white in widths of 92 cm (36 in) and 115 cm (45 in). This fabric can be purchased from almost any fabric shop or department store. It will be also available by mail order (see page 7).

FABRICS

Thin and thick cotton, georgette, polyester lining fabric, polyester crepes and habutai silk.

COTTON THREAD

Thick cotton thread (white buttonhole thread is ideal) is used for making stamens for flowers such as Freesias, Fuchsias, Gypsophila, etc. Cotton thread of any sort (use the cheapest available) is also needed for binding stamens and petals to the stem: any colour can be used for this. By using cotton thread you use less glue.

STEM TAPE

This is used by florists, and is needed for covering wires for stems. It is made from paper impregnated with adhesive, and comes in various shades of green. It can be bought from craft shops or florists. It is also used to make stamens, to join together two or three wires to make a thicker stem, or to join leaves to make a set.

When covering wires for leaf and petal supports, use half or one-third width stem tape. To cut the width of the stem tape, wrap a piece approximately 60 cm (24 in) long around your hand. Cut it lengthwise into two or three strips (depending on whether you require half or one-third width stem tape). Do not cut it any thinner, as it will tear.

15

Materials

WIRE

Wrapped in stem tape, wire serves as stems for flowers, and as petal and leaf supports. Wire comes in different gauges and can be bought at any craft shop. The sizes used are 100 mm (no. 19), 71 mm (no. 22), and 46 mm (no. 26). The higher the number, the thinner the wire.

GLUE

Glue is needed for sticking the petals on and for attaching wire supports to leaves and petals. A clear, quick-drying adhesive with a small nozzle is recommended. PVA can be used applied with a cotton bud or matchstick, but dries very slowly.

COTTON WOOL

This is used to swell the base of calyxes and to form the inner core of flowers and buds. It also makes stamens. (Buy the cheapest sort.)

ARROWROOT OR CORNSTARCH

This is used for starching fabric. All fabrics must be starched before being cut, to prevent the fabric from fraying and to maintain the original shape of the petals and leaves.

Do not confuse cornstarch with cornflour. Both are made from almost the same ingredients, but cornflour has undergone a slightly different process during manufacture and leaves a film on the fabric when used, which affects the results of dyeing and tinting.

PVA MULTIGLUE

This is added to starch to help prevent the fabric from fraying. It is also used for making stamens. It is white in colour, but dries clear and can be bought from any stationer's.

POLYFILLA

Polyfilla of any sort is used for making stamens.

BLOTTING PAPER

Used for absorbing excess dyes from petals, which are left to dry on it.

PLASTIC TUBING

This is an electrical sleeving, and is available in different diameters. Those used in this book are 4 mm ($\frac{1}{8}$ in) and 6 mm ($\frac{1}{4}$ in) in diameter. A hardware or electrical shop should stock them. By passing wire through the tube, stems can be made thicker.

COLD-WATER DYES

For dyeing petals to the required colour. They can be bought in craft shops.

FIXING AGENTS

Use a cold fix to help make colours permanent.

FABRIC PAINTS

These are diluted with water, depending on the colour and texture required. The solution is brushed on the petals, where it fills in the grain of the fabric and makes the petals look thicker (especially silk) for Freesias, Crocuses, etc. The paints can be bought in craft shops or department stores.

FELT-TIP PENS

These are used to make lines on stamen strips to give the appearance of anthers, as well as spots on lilies, and all markings on petals. They must only be used on petals after shaping.

DOUBLE-SIDED CREPE PAPER

This is used as a substitute for stamens.

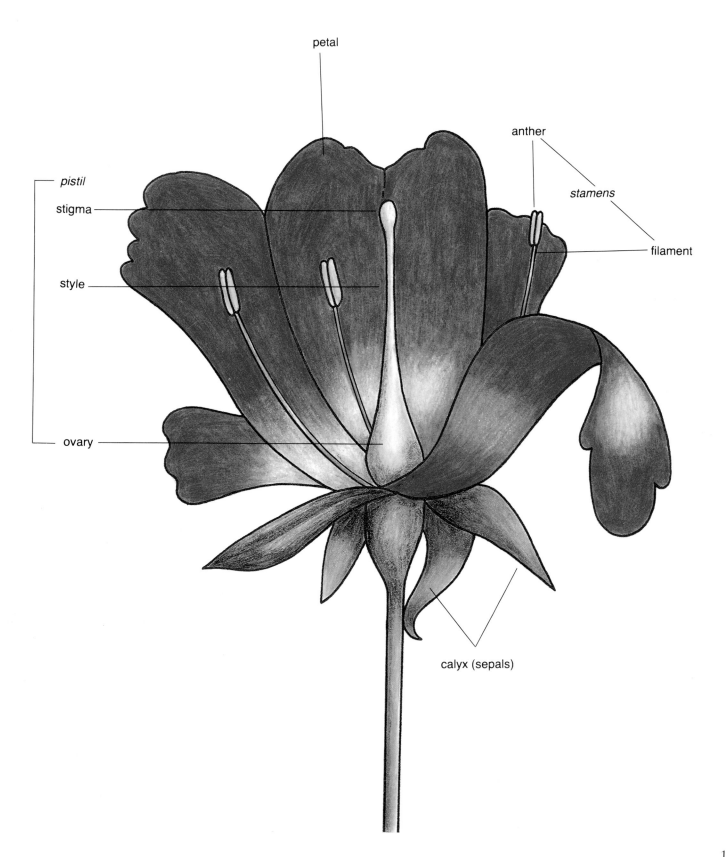

petal

anther

stamens

filament

pistil

stigma

style

ovary

calyx (sepals)

Best wishes

PREPARING THE FABRIC

Fabrics must be starched before cutting out petals, leaves and calyxes. Use the following method.

Materials

275 ml (10 fl oz) cold water
1 level tablespoon of arrowroot or cornstarch
3 tablespoons cold water
1 teaspoon PVA multiglue

Method

Heat water in a pan to boiling point. Mix arrowroot or cornstarch with three tablespoons of cold water. Add the mixture to boiling water, stirring until it turns clear. Take the pan off the heat and add the PVA multiglue, stirring thoroughly until the mixture turns white. Allow to cool before applying the starch to the fabric.

Application to fabric

To apply starch, lay the fabric flat on a laminated work-top or table. Apply the starch with a clean brush, starting from the middle of the fabric and brushing outwards to either side. This is to avoid stretching the fabric. Moisten a piece of clean cloth with water and wipe away any excess starch: this also helps to distribute the starch evenly and to disperse bubbles. Allow the fabric to dry completely before lifting off. It is now ready to cut out.

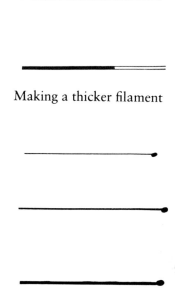

Making a thicker filament

Larger Polyfilla stamens can be made by dipping them into the paste again.

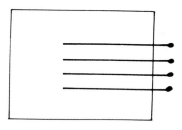

While drying, position Polyfilla stamens so that they do not touch each other or the surface

MAKING SMALL YELLOW STAMENS

Materials

Polyfilla
PVA multiglue
Water
Yellow fabric paint
Cotton buttonhole thread
Arrowroot or cornstarch

Method

Mix 1 tablespoon of made-up starch (cooked), 1 teaspoon of PVA multiglue and a touch of yellow paint, depending on the shade of yellow required. Cut a few long lengths of cotton thread for making the filaments. Dip your finger into the mixture and run the cotton thread through your finger and thumb, making sure it is thoroughly coated. Hang it in a line to dry. When it is completely dry, cut the stiffened cotton thread into 5 cm (2 in) lengths. To make a thicker filament, use two strands of cotton thread together and apply stiffening.

To make the anthers (stamens' heads), mix 1 level teaspoon of polyfilla, ½ teaspoon of multiglue and ½ teaspoon of water into a soft paste. Add a small amount of yellow fabric paint, again depending on the shade of yellow required. Dip the tips of each piece of filament (stiffened cotton thread) into the paste, making sure it picks up a tiny blob. Now place it on a flat plate or cutting board to dry, allowing the blobs to suspend without touching. Leave to dry for about 10–15 minutes until hard. Dip it in the paste again if you need a larger anther. The deeper you dip the filament into the paste, the larger the anther will be. Make into small bundles with the stamens and store for later use. You can make stamens in any colour by mixing the appropriate colour of dye or fabric paint into the paste.

MAKING STAMENS AND PISTILS FROM STEM TAPE

Materials

Thin wire (no. 26)
Light green stem tape
Brown stem tape

Method

Cut a few thin wires in 64 mm (2½ in) lengths. Cover the wires with half-width green stem tape. Cut a piece of brown stem tape 10 mm × 13 mm (⅜ in × ½ in) and wrap it around one end of the covered wire.

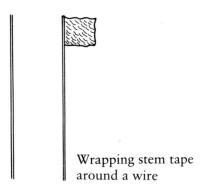

Wrapping stem tape around a wire

Now bend it into the shape required.

To make the pistil, cut the thin wires (no. 26) into 76 mm (3 in) lengths. Cover the wires with half-width green stem tape. Now bend the tip of the wire over twice and wrap a piece of brown stem tape around and over it, making it into a flat round shape.

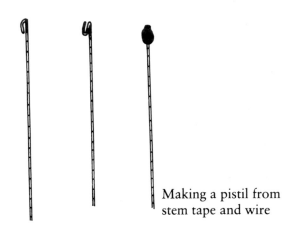

Making a pistil from stem tape and wire

There are several shapes of these stamens in different species of Lily.

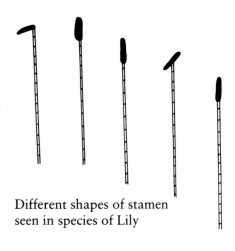

Different shapes of stamen seen in species of Lily

The anthers are in several different colours. If you are unsure what colours to use, refer to the real flowers. To make coloured stamens, use white stem tape which can be coloured the desired shade using felt-tip pens.

MAKING LARGE STAMENS AND PISTILS FROM COTTON WOOL

Materials

Cotton wool
PVA multiglue
Dye (colour required)
Thin wire (no. 26)
Stem tape (colour required)

Method

Thin out a piece of cotton wool by separating it into thin layers. Cover the thin wires with half-width stem tape and cut into required lengths. Cut a small strip of cotton wool about 6 mm ($\frac{1}{4}$ in) × 13 mm ($\frac{1}{2}$ in) and wrap it around one end of the covered wire. Roll it very firmly between the forefinger and thumb.

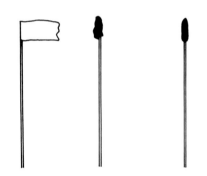

Making a cotton wool stamen and pistil

Mix 1 teaspoon of PVA multiglue with the colour of dye or paint required and 1 teaspoon of water, stirring it well with a small brush. Apply the mixture to the cotton wool with the brush, covering it completely. Place on a flat plate or cutting board to dry, with the stamens' heads suspended and without touching. Leave to dry overnight.

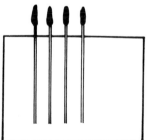

Leave stamens to dry so that they do not touch each other

The shapes are usually round or flat rectangles. The pistils are made by the same method, except that most are round and flat or just round. To make the stamen or pistil flat, after it has dried, place it on a piece of cardboard on a hard surface and hit it with a small hammer or the metal handle of a knife.

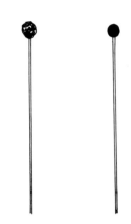

Different shapes of pistil

MAKING PAPER STAMENS FROM DOUBLE-SIDED CREPE PAPER

Double-sided crepe paper has two colours, one on each side of the paper. It is available in assorted colours such as yellow/cream, dark green/pale green, etc., in sheets measuring 24·8 cm ($9\frac{3}{4}$ in) × 122 cm (48 in). It can be purchased at any craft shop. Paper stamens make a perfect substitute for flower stamens, as you will see from the colour plates. One flower can have as many as 30–40 stamens. One of my main reasons for using double-sided crepe paper is that it looks just as effective as the real stamens and is also very economical to use.

One point to note is, when you are making slits on the stamen strip, it must be cut through on the vertical grain.

Making paper stamens: cutting the strip

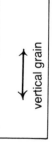

vertical grain

Cut the size of a strip required for the stamens. Use a felt-tip pen to draw a line across the edge of the strip. The drawn line represents the anthers. Make the slits required, using the blade of the scissors to curve the fringe with the drawn line showing at the top.

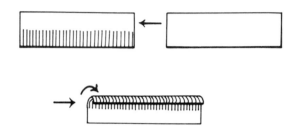

Cut a fringe along one edge of the strip

On stamens where both sides of the fringe can be seen, lines have to be drawn on both sides of the edge.

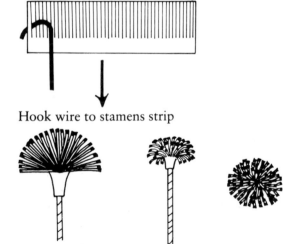

Hook wire to stamens strip

Stamens where both sides of the fringe can be seen

MAKING TEMPLATES

To make templates, first make a tracing of each part of the flower pattern, making sure you include the arrows shown. Then paste the tracings on a thin piece of cardboard and cut them out. Each set of templates should be placed in an envelope and labelled. They are now ready for cutting out your flowers.

CUTTING OUT

Place templates on the starched fabric so that the arrows are running parallel with the lengthwise grain of the fabric (use the selvedge as a guide). Cut petals, leaves and calyxes diagonally, to allow flexibility in the shaping. With patterns where the petals are joined in a round shape, e.g. Carnation, the template can be placed in any direction on the fabric. With thin fabrics, eg. silks, cut two or more small petals at a time.

DYEING AND TINTING

All handmade flowers, even white ones, are highlighted by careful shading in an appropriate colour. Recommended methods of colouring are cold-water dyes, fabric paints and felt-tip pens. This process of colouring matches the colours precisely and gives it a more natural effect.

MIXING COLD-WATER DYES

Ingredients (to make up a concentrated dye)

1 tin cold-water dye
0·14 litre ($\frac{1}{4}$ pt) cold water
1 teaspoon cold fix

Method

Heat the water and add fixative (cold fix). Stir until the fixative dissolves. Allow the mixture to cool. Empty the tin of dye into a jug and pour in the fixative mixture. Stir thoroughly and store in an airtight jar or bottle.

APPLYING COLOUR TO THE FLOWERS

To dye or tint, a number of items are required:

Blotting paper	Pair of tweezers
Teaspoon	A fine and a medium
Dishes for dyes	artist's brush
Cotton wool	Detergent water (1 drop
Large white plate	of detergent liquid to
	$\frac{1}{2}$ cup of water)

Spoon enough dye into a dish to colour the required number of petals. Shades can be varied by adding water a teaspoon at a time. Every teaspoon of water makes the dye one shade lighter. You should get fifteen to sixteen shades from one tin of dye.

Use a pair of tweezers to dip the petals, a few at a time, into the dye. Lay them on a plate for about one to two minutes for the dye to be fully absorbed, then transfer to a sheet of blotting paper to dry. If you need to tint the edges of the petals, use a fine brush to apply the colour sparingly, and touch the parts to be tinted while they are still damp so that the colours blend in. By using a brush you can blend in more than one shade on the petal.

To dye the edges of the petal only, first moisten the whole petal with a piece of cotton wool dipped in detergent water and then dip the petal edge into the dye solution, or use a small brush to apply the dye.

Discard any left-over dye, unless it is stored in a separate container to be re-used in a few days.

Recommended colours (dyes)

Mexican red   (red)
Camellia   (deep pink)
Mandarin   (orange)
Leaf green   (green)
Bahama blue   (blue)

These are the base colours essential to make up a variety of others. They should all be made up in a concentrated solution to enable you to get 15–16 shades from one tin of cold-water dye, with the exception of leaf green. There is no reason why you cannot experiment with mixing different colours to get a specific colour of your choice.

MIXING FABRIC PAINTS

Ingredients

Fabric paint
Water
Cold water dye (concentrated)

Method

When using fabric paints, there are some variations. Paints can be mixed with either water or cold water dyes to get a specific colour.

To prepare fabric paints with water, mix five parts of water to one part of fabric paint. Add the water a little at a time to make sure the paint is fully dissolved.

Depending on the shade required, fabric paints can also be mixed with concentrated dyes after water has been added to the paint. Fabric paints are ideal for producing a thick-set petal, such as for Freesias and Crocuses. It fills in the grain of the fabric, making the petals look thicker, giving the beautiful texture of a life-like flower, especially when using habutai silk or other thin fabrics.

The paint must be diluted by adding water gradually, using a small brush to stir it. This breaks up the sediments or gel. Before applying paint, the petals must first be dampened with cotton wool dipped in detergent water. This helps them to accept the paint more readily and evenly.

Recommended colours (fabric paints)

Yellow (no. 1)
White

SHAPING

After starching, cutting and dyeing (if desired) fabric, heat tools on an electric cooker between heat settings 3–4. Some fabrics, such as polyester lining, may need a lower heat setting of about 2–3. Do not let heated tools rest too long on flower parts while shaping, as delicate fabrics may be scorched. Heat only the tools required, taking care that the handles do not touch the heated plate or ring. Moisten the parts of the flower on a damp cloth, place them on the foam rubber and shape accordingly. The parts of the flower must be dampened before curling, creasing and veining, to give them a permanent shape. Do not over-dampen the petals, as they will stretch and fray. Trim off any frayed or rough sections before finishing off.

A gas cooker may also be used, by placing a baking tray or an old baking tin over the flame. Make sure that the handles of the tools are not exposed directly to the flames, as they are made from wood. It is not advisable to place the tools directly on gas flames.

Step-by-step guide to making the rose

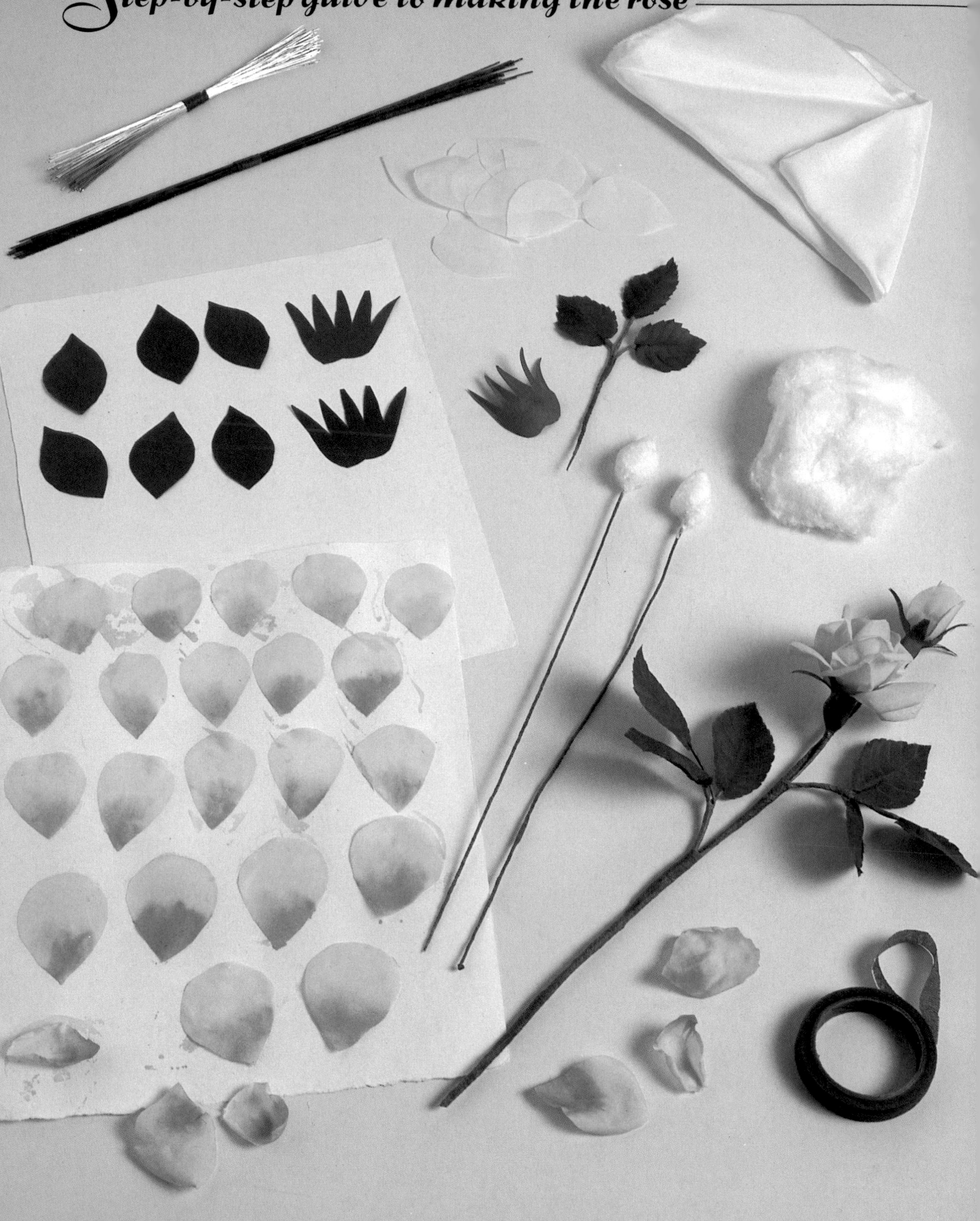

The step-by-step photographs show the making of a rose, which encompasses all the different techniques you are likely to need in making all the flowers in the book.

1. The petals may be dyed as shown here. These petals are cut from white Habutai silk and dyed with yellow fabric paint; the orange base is dyed using mandarin dye.

2. The tools are heated on a hot plate on a 2–3 setting. Keep the wooden handles away from the heat.

3. The medium and small petals are moistened and the tips are curled using the spade marker.

4. The large petals' tips are curled with both the tip of the spade marker and the curler goffer.

5. The hollows in the petals are made with the ball goffer. Make a light hollow on the large petals. The depth of the hollow depends on the pressure applied: the greater the pressure, the deeper the hollow.

6. The leaves are veined using the spade marker. The calyx is shaped with the spade marker and the ball goffer – the spade marker is used on the pointed ends of the calyx, and the ball goffer makes the hollow at the base.

7. The stem wires are covered with full-width stem tape. The leaf support wires are covered with half-width stem tape.

8. The inner core, or heart, of the flower and bud are formed with cotton wool.

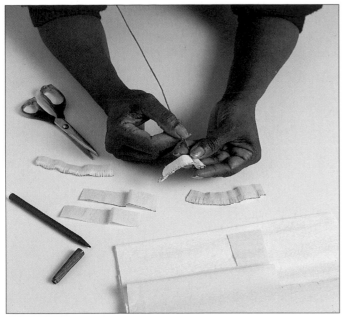

9. To make an open-centred rose, paper stamens are used instead of cotton wool. Roll the strip of stamens around the stem with the curled edge falling inwards.

10. The bud is made up of five small petals. A length of cotton thread is wound around the stem, ready to bind the petals. The first petal is glued closely around the cotton wool. The second petal is glued opposite the first, and the remaining three in an alternating pattern. Each petal must be bound with cotton thread before attaching the next.

11. A piece of cotton wool is wrapped around the stem to form the base for the calyx, and this is covered with stem tape. The calyx is glued on and a length of cotton thread is wrapped around the neck of the calyx to swell the base. The join between the calyx and stem is covered with stem tape.

12. The edges of the leaves are serrated with a pair of sharp scissors.

13. The thin covered wires are glued at the back of the leaves. Three leaves are joined to make a set.

14. The inner part of the rose is made up in the same way as the bud. The five medium petals are then glued on, spacing and binding them around the small petals.

15. The large petals are glued and bound around the medium petals in an alternating pattern. The rose calyx is formed like the bud calyx.

16. Stem tape is used to join the leaves and bud to the rose stem. The rose and bud are complete.

Part 2

The Flowers

(For one flower)

Petals
Polyester lining fabric (pink)

Stamens
Yellow double-sided crêpe paper
Black felt-tip pen

Stem
1 wire (no. 22), 30 cm (12 in) length
Light green stem tape

Tools required
Spade marker; 19 mm ($\frac{3}{4}$ in) ball goffer

anemone petals
cut 1

anemone stamens   cut 1

1. Cut one large and one small set of petals (six petals in each set). Cut one strip of double-sided crêpe paper 76 mm × 19 mm (3 in × $\frac{3}{4}$ in) for stamens. Draw a thin line across the edge on both sides of the stamen strip. Make slits to half-way down by cutting through the line. Use the blade of the scissors to curve the edge of the stamens over. Cover the stem wire (no. 22) with stem tape. Bend the tip of the wire and hook one end of the stamens into it. Glue along the lower edge of the stamen strip and roll it evenly around the stem wire.

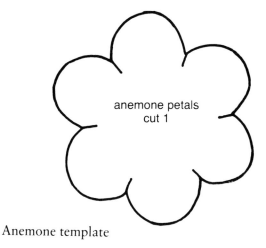

anemone petals
cut 1

Anemone template

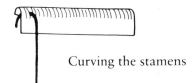

Curving the stamens

The stamens complete

2. Moisten petals and place on the 13 mm ($\frac{1}{2}$ in) foam rubber. Make three veins on each petal using the spade marker. Moisten the centre of the petals and make a light hollow with the ball goffer. Use the black felt-tip pen to mark lines in the centre of both large and small sets of petals.

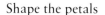

Shape the petals

Mark the centre of the petals

33

3. To assemble the flower, make a slit in the centre of the petals large enough for the underside of the stamens to pass through. Glue under the stamens and pass the stem through the small set of petals and stick. Now glue under the small petals and pass the stem through the large set of petals. Wrap a piece of stem tape around the stem under the flower to tidy the join.

The Anemone complete

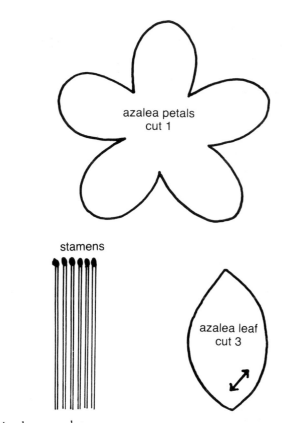

azalea petals
cut 1

stamens

azalea leaf
cut 3

Azalea template

(For one flower and three leaves)

Petals
White habutai silk

Stamens
7 orange stamens
Cotton wool

Stem
1 thin wire (no. 26), 15 cm (6 in) length
Green stem tape

Leaves
Green cotton
3 thin wires (no. 26), 76 mm (3 in) length

Dyes
Mandarin dye

Tools required
Spade marker

---

1. Cut one set of petals (five petals in each set) from white silk, and three leaves from green cotton. Dye petals the required colour by mixing mandarin dye with water. Allow to dry.

2. Moisten petals and place on the 13 mm (½ in) foam rubber. Press the edges of the petals with the spade marker to make a very tiny curl. Moisten the petals again and make three veins on each petal. Now moisten the centre of the petals, turn them over and place on the 51 mm (2 in) foam rubber. Using the pointed tip of the spade marker, press deep in the centre of the petals so that the centre forms a point.

Curl the petal edges

Make three veins on each petal

Form a point at the centre

3. Moisten the leaves and make veins with the spade marker. Cover the three thin wires (no. 26) with half-width stem tape, then glue these in the centre at the back of the leaves 13 mm ($\frac{1}{2}$ in) away from the tip. Join the leaves to make a set.

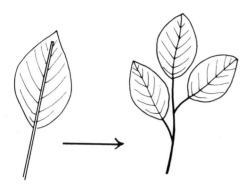

Join the leaves in a set

4. Cover stem wire (no. 26) with stem tape. Bind the seven stamens 13 mm ($\frac{1}{2}$ in) from the end of the stem with stem tape. The stamens should be 25 mm (1 in) in height. Make a small slit in the centre of the petals and pass the stem through, allowing the flower petals to rest between the stamens and stem. Wrap a tiny piece of cotton wool around the stem where the stamens meet it. Cover the cotton wool with stem tape. Put glue on top of the covered cotton wool and stick the flower petals on. Attach the leaves to the stem about 76 mm (3 in) below the flower using stem tape.

Binding the stamens

The Azalea complete

Carnation

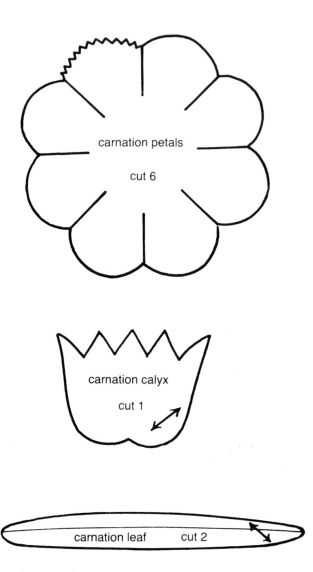

Carnation templates

(For one flower and two leaves)

Petals
White habutai silk

Calyx
Thick green cotton
Cotton wool

Stem
Coarse wire (no. 19), 31 cm (12 in)
length
Green stem tape

Leaves
Thick green cotton
2 thin wires (no. 26), 13 cm (5 in)
length

Dyes
Required colours

Tools required
Chaser goffer; spade marker, 13 mm ($\frac{1}{2}$ in) and 19 mm ($\frac{3}{4}$ in), ball goffer

1. Cut six sets of petals (eight petals in each set) from white silk. Cut one calyx and two leaves from green cotton. To cut the petals, cut a round piece of silk a little larger than the pattern and make three folds so that it becomes one petal. Cut a curve around the edge, serrate the edges and snip off the folded corner before opening the petals.

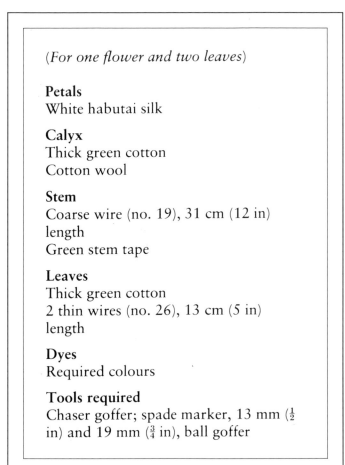

Fold the petals

1st fold

2nd fold   3rd fold

Serrate the edges

folded petal

clipped-off edge

2. Mix dye to the required colour. Dye four sets of petals a little darker for the inner petals, and the remaining two lighter for the outer petals. Allow to dry. Moisten the inner petals and place on the 13 mm ($\frac{1}{2}$ in) foam rubber. Make creases with the chaser goffer by pressing the tool on the edge of the petals and pulling down to the centre, releasing pressure as you pull. Make 13 mm ($\frac{1}{2}$ in) slits between the petals after creasing. Moisten the centre of the petals and place on the 51 mm (2 in) foam rubber. Make a deep hollow with the 13 mm ($\frac{1}{2}$ in) ball goffer, creating a bell shape. Make creases on the outer petals, moisten the centre and turn them over. Make a light hollow with the 19 mm ($\frac{3}{4}$ in) ball goffer, again making 13 mm ($\frac{1}{2}$ in) slits after creasing the petals.

39

3. Moisten the calyx and place on the 13 mm (½ in) foam rubber. Use the pointed tip of the spade marker to press lightly on all five points of the calyx. Turn the calyx over, using the 19 mm (¾ in) ball goffer to make a hollow by working the tool from side to side. Use the tip of the spade marker for the leaves by pressing the pointed tip of the tool from the tip to the base of the leaf, keeping a straight line all the way down. Cover the two wires (no. 26) with half-width stem tape and glue in the centre at the back of each leaf, 13 mm (½ in) away from the tip.

Create a bell shape

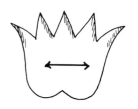

Shaping the calyx

4. Cover stem wire (no. 19) with stem tape. Wrap a piece of cotton wool no more than 19 mm (¾ in) deep around one end of the stem. Half-way, bend the tip of the wire to secure the cotton wool. Mould the cotton wool into a bud shape with your fingers and cover with stem tape.

The leaf shape

5. Glue the tip and base of the cotton wool bud; pass the stem through one of the inner (cup shaped) petals, stick it down firmly on to the bud and cover it completely. Now glue around the first set of inner petals about 19 mm (¾ in) above the base, applying the glue sparingly. Slip the second set of petals on and stick them by squeezing gently with the palm of your hand. Repeat with the third set of petals. Apply glue to and stick the fourth set of petals, but do not squeeze. The outer petals are glued at the base only, and arranged alternately. Wrap a piece of cotton wool around the stem under the petals to swell the base, so that the calyx can be wrapped around it and only overlap a little. Before covering the cotton wool base with stem tape, make sure that the calyx can go around it. Now glue on the calyx. Tidy the join between the stem and calyx with stem tape. Attach the leaves about 76 mm (3 in) below the calyx, facing each other.

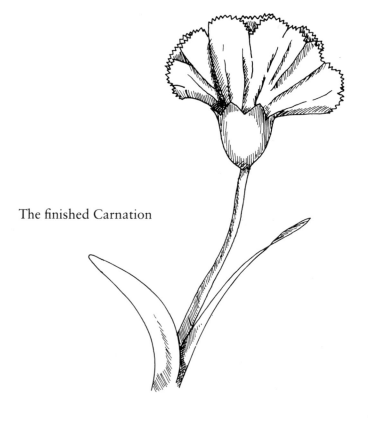

The finished Carnation

(*For one flower and six leaves*)

Flower sepals
Cream polyester (lining fabric) or cotton
6 thin wires (no. 26) 64 mm (2½ in) lengths
White stem tape
Cotton thread

Stamens
Yellow double-sided crêpe paper

Leaves
Green polyester (lining fabric) or cotton
4 thin wires (no. 26), 51 mm (2 in) lengths
2 thin wires (no. 26), 38 mm (1½ in) lengths

Stem
1 medium wire (no. 22), 30 cm (12 in) length
Green stem tape

Tools required
Spade marker

1. Cut six flower sepals from cream fabric, and six leaves (two of each size) from green fabric. Cut two strips of double-sized crêpe paper, 51 mm (2 in) × 19 mm (¾ in) for the inner stamens and 25 mm (1 in) × 19 mm (¾ in) for the outer stamens. Make slits half-way down the inner stamens and curve the fringe with the blade of the scissors. Cover the stem wire (no. 22) with green stem tape, bend over the tip of the wire and hook over one end of the inner stamens. Glue the lower edge of the strip and roll evenly around the stem wire. Make 13 mm (½ in) slits on the outer stamens and slightly curve the fringe. Glue along the lower edge and roll evenly around and over the inner stamens, allowing the curve to fall inwards.

Clematis templates

inner stamens   cut 1

outer stamens

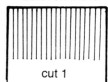

cut 1

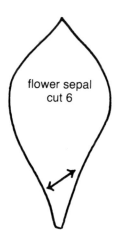

flower sepal
cut 6

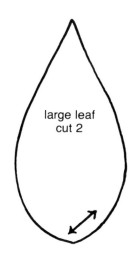

large leaf
cut 2

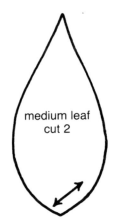

medium leaf
cut 2

small leaf
cut 2

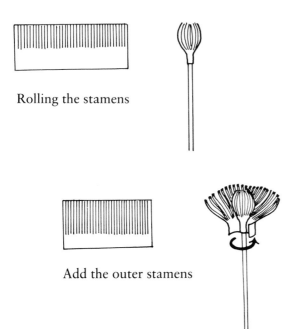

Rolling the stamens

Add the outer stamens

3. Moisten the leaves and place on the 13 mm ($\frac{1}{2}$ in) foam rubber. Make veins on all the leaves using the spade marker. Cover the thin wires (no. 26) with half-width green stem tape and glue these in the centre at the back of each leaf 13 mm ($\frac{1}{2}$ in) away from the tip. The 51 mm (2 in) wires are for the large and medium leaves, the 38 mm ($1\frac{1}{2}$ in) for the smaller leaves.

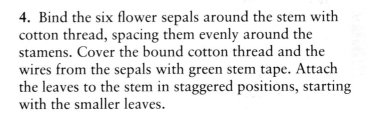

The Clematis leaf

2. Moisten flower sepals and place on the 13 mm ($\frac{1}{2}$ in) foam rubber. Use the spade marker to press and make a very short pull on the edges, starting with the centre point of the sepal. Turn the sepals over and make five veins on each. Cover the six thin wires (no. 26) with half-width white stem tape and glue these at the back of each sepal, 13 mm ($\frac{1}{2}$ in) away from the tip and extending 13 mm ($\frac{1}{2}$ in) below the base. Squeeze about 6 mm ($\frac{1}{4}$ in) on the base of the sepals around the support wire before the glue dries to secure the sepals.

4. Bind the six flower sepals around the stem with cotton thread, spacing them evenly around the stamens. Cover the bound cotton thread and the wires from the sepals with green stem tape. Attach the leaves to the stem in staggered positions, starting with the smaller leaves.

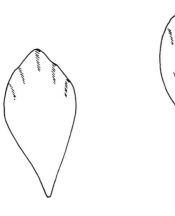

Shape for the sepal   Add the support wire

The Clematis complete

(For one flower)

Petals
White habutai silk

Calyx
Thin green cotton

Stem
1 medium wire (no. 22), 25 cm (10 in) length
Green stem tape

Dyes
Bahama blue

Tools required
Spade marker; 6 mm ($\frac{1}{4}$ in) and 13 mm ($\frac{1}{2}$ in) ball goffers

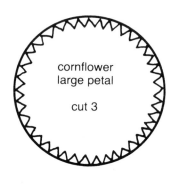

Cornflower templates

1. Cut three large and three small sets of petals, and one calyx. Serrate the edges of the petals using a pair of pinking shears. Dye the petals bahama blue by dipping the petals in the dye. Allow to dry. Make a slit in the centre of all the petals for the stem to pass through.

2. Moisten the small sets of petals and place on the 13 mm ($\frac{1}{2}$ in) foam rubber. Make veins with the spade marker and make slits all around the petals. Moisten the centre of the petals and place on the 51 mm (2 in) foam rubber. Press the 6 mm ($\frac{1}{4}$ in) ball goffer on the petals to make a deep hollow.

3. Moisten the large petals and make veins and slits like those on the smaller ones. Now moisten the centres, turn them over and make a shallow hollow in the centre with the 13 mm ($\frac{1}{2}$ in) ball goffer. Moisten the calyx and make veins using the spade marker. Make a small slit in the centre for the stem to pass through.

Dividing the petals

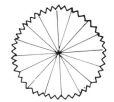
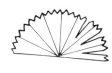

Make a deep hollow
in the petals

Shaping the petals

Make a slit in the centre

4. Cover the stem wire (no. 22) with stem tape.
Wrap a small piece of cotton wool (the size of a
small pea) around one end of the stem. Half-way,
bend the tip of the stem over to secure the cotton
wool. Cover this with stem tape. Glue the cotton
bud at the tip and the base. Pass the stem through
one of the small sets of petals and stick it closely
around the cotton bud. Now glue at the base and
half-way up the petals, then slip the second set of
petals through. Repeat for the third set. Now glue
the base of the petals and add one of the large sets of
petals. Repeat for the two remaining sets. Glue and
stick on the calyx.

The Cornflower complete

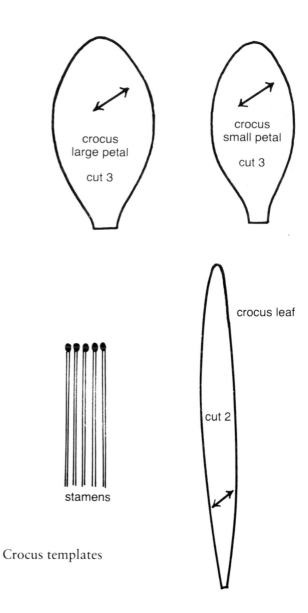

(For one flower and one leaf)

Petals
White habutai silk
Brown felt-tip pen

Stamens
5 orange stamens (stem tape stamens 37 mm ($1\frac{1}{2}$ in) length
Cotton thread

Stem
1 wire (no. 22), 15 cm (6 in) length
Plastic tube 7 mm ($\frac{1}{4}$ in) diameter, 138 mm ($5\frac{1}{2}$ in) length
Green stem tape

Leaf
Green cotton
1 thin wire (no. 26), 76 mm (3 in) length

Fabric paint
Yellow

Tools required
Spade marker; 19 mm ($\frac{3}{4}$ in); ball goffers

crocus large petal
cut 3

crocus small petal
cut 3

crocus leaf

cut 2

stamens

Crocus templates

1. Cut three large and three small petals from white habutai silk and one leaf from green cotton. Mix the yellow fabric paint with water to get the required colour, brush it on the petals and allow to dry. Moisten petals and place on the 13 mm ($\frac{1}{2}$ in) foam rubber. Lightly curl the edges of the petals with the spade marker. Make a hollow on the petals with the 19 mm ($\frac{3}{4}$ in) ball goffer, pressing and pulling the tool from the base to the tip of the petals. Shape both large and small petals in the same way. Moisten the leaf using the pointed tip of the spade marker; press and pull from the tip to the base. Shape the calyx in the same way as the carnation. Cover the 76 mm (3 in) wire (no. 26) with half-width stem tape and glue it at the back of the leaf, 13 mm ($\frac{1}{2}$ in) away from the tip.

2. Mark lines on the base of the petals with the brown felt-tip pen. Cover stem wire (no. 22) with

Mark lines on the petals

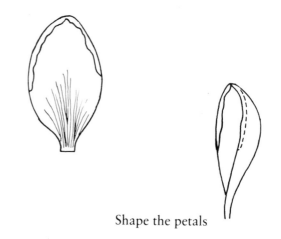

Shape the petals

stem tape and bind the five stamens 13 mm ($\frac{1}{2}$ in) down the stem using cotton thread. Half-way, bend the tip of the stem over to secure the stamens, and then complete the binding. The height of the stamens should be 25 mm (1 in). Cover the binding cotton thread with stem tape. Glue the filaments together.

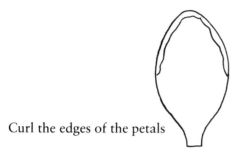

Curl the edges of the petals

3. Glue the bases of the larger petals and stick them around the stem where it meets the stamens. Now glue and stick the remaining petals between the large petals, setting them alternately. Apply some glue around the stem under the petals, and pass the stem wire through the plastic tube to make a thicker stem. Cover with stem tape. The leaf can either be left independent or can be joined to the stem tape.

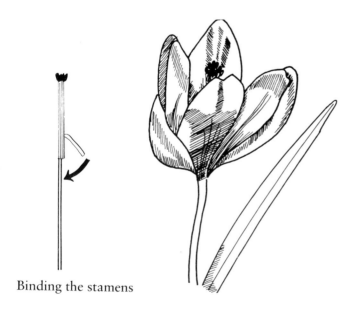

Binding the stamens

The Crocus complete

Daisy————————————————————————

(For one flower and one leaf)

Petals
White cotton

Stamens
Yellow double-sided crêpe paper
Brown felt-tip pen

Calyx
Dark green cotton or polyester lining

Leaf
Dark green cotton or polyester lining
1 thin wire (no. 26), 50 mm (2 in)
length

Stem
1 medium wire (no. 22), 30 cm (12 in)
length
Dark green stem tape

Tools required
Spade marker; 13 mm ($\frac{1}{2}$ in) ball goffer

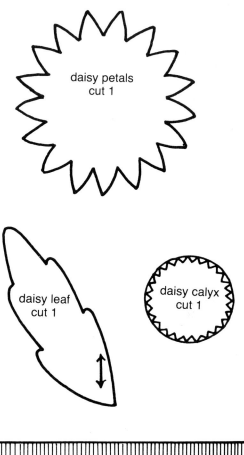

Daisy templates

1. Cut one set of petals, one leaf, one strip of double-sided crêpe paper for stamens 76 mm (3 in) × 13 mm ($\frac{1}{2}$ in), and one calyx. Draw a line across one edge of the stamen strip using brown felt-tip pen. Make slits half-way down the strip and curve the fringe with the blade of the scissors so that the felt-tip line shows on top. Cover the stem wire (no. 22) with stem tape. Bend the tip of the stem wire to hook over one end of the stamens. Glue the lower edge of the stamen strip and roll it evenly around the stem with the curved edge of the fringe falling outwards.

2. Moisten the leaf and make veins using the spade marker. Cover the 50 mm (2 in) wire (no. 26) with half-width stem tape and glue this in the centre at the back of the leaf, 13 mm ($\frac{1}{2}$ in) away from the tip. Make veins on the calyx and a slit in the centre for the stem to pass through.

Shape the fringe

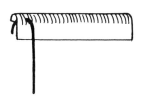

Roll so that the fringe falls outwards

3. Moisten the petals and place on the 13 mm (½ in) foam rubber. Make veins on top and between the petals. With a sharp pair of scissors, make slits between each petal about 13 mm (½ in) away from the centre. Turn it over and press the ball goffer in the centre to make a hollow. Now make a slit in the centre of the petals to pass the stem through.

4. Glue under the stamens. Pass the stem through the set of petals, sticking it to the stamens. Now glue on the calyx. Wrap a piece of stem tape around the stem to tidy between the edges of the calyx and the stem. Attach the leaf about 76 mm (3 in) below the flower.

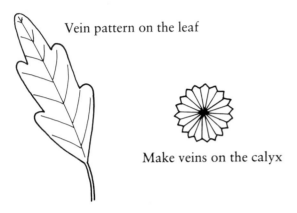

Vein pattern on the leaf

Make veins on the calyx

Make a slit in the centre of the petals

The Daisy complete

(For one spray of 37 leaves)

Leaves
Green cotton or polyester lining fabric
32 thin wires (no. 26), 25 mm (1 in)
lengths

Stems
4 thin wires (no. 26), 100 mm (4 in)
lengths
1 thin wire (no. 26), 175 mm (7 in)
length
1 medium wire (no. 22), 75 mm (3 in)
length
Green stem tape

Tools required
Spade marker

Maidenhair Fern templates

4. Make four sets of three leaves by joining one small leaf and two medium leaves with one-third width stem tape. Make four further sets of five leaves by joining two medium and two large leaves to the 100 mm (4 in) covered wires attached to the small leaves.

5. To make up the spray, add four medium leaves to the 175 mm (7 in) covered wire with the small leaf, again using one-third width stem tape for attaching the leaves. Now attach the four sets of three leaves and the four sets of five leaves. Use half-width stem tape to join the 75 mm (3 in) medium wire (no. 22) to thicken the lower part of the stem.

1. Cut nine small, twenty medium and eight large leaves from green fabric. Serrate the edges of the leaves using pinking shears.

2. Moisten leaves and place on the 13 mm ($\frac{1}{2}$ in) foam rubber or a tea towel folded into four layers. Make four vertical veins on each leaf.

3. Cover all the thin wires (no. 26) with one-third width stem tape. Glue the 25 mm (1 in) covered wires to four small, twenty medium and eight large leaves. Glue the 100 mm (4 in) covered wires to four small leaves and the 175 mm (7 in) wires to the remaining small leaf 6 mm ($\frac{1}{4}$ in) away from the tip on all the leaves.

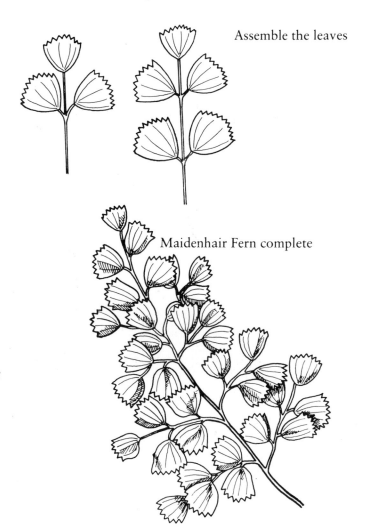

Assemble the leaves

Maidenhair Fern complete

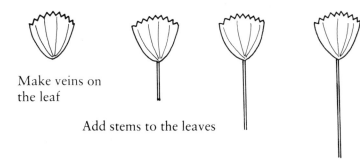

Make veins on
the leaf

Add stems to the leaves

Freesia ————————————————————————

(*For one flower*)

Petals
White habutai silk

Stamens
6 orange stamens
Cotton thread

Calyx
White habutai silk

Stem
1 medium wire (no. 22), 20 cm (8 in) length
Green stem tape

Dyes and fabric paint
Yellow fabric paint
Leaf-green dye

Tools required
Spade marker

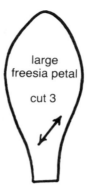 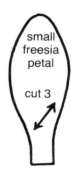

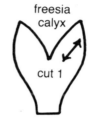 

Freesia templates   stamens

1. Cut three large and three small petals and one calyx from white silk. Dye the petals by mixing yellow fabric paint with water until it reaches the shade of yellow required. For the base of the petals, spoon a small amount of the mixed fabric paint into a separate dish and add a few drops of leaf-green dye to make a lime-green colour. Brush on the mixed yellow fabric paint so that it covers two-thirds of each petal. With a separate brush apply the lime-green colour to the base of the petals immediately, so that the colours blend in. Add some more leaf-green dye to the lime-green and dye the calyx. Allow to dry.

2. Moisten the petals and place on the 13 mm ($\frac{1}{2}$ in) foam rubber. Press with the flat side of the spade marker to curl the edges of the petals lightly. Turn the petals over and lightly press the pointed tip of the spade marker from near the tip to about 19 mm ($\frac{3}{4}$ in) down the petal. Moisten the calyx and place on the 13 mm ($\frac{1}{2}$ in) foam rubber. Using the pointed tip of the spade marker, press and pull to about 13 mm ($\frac{1}{2}$ in) from the base of the calyx on both points.

Curl the edges of the petals   Shape the centre of the petals

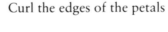

Colour the petals   lime-green

3. Apply glue sparingly to the bases of the petals, and stick them one over the other. Starting with a large petal, glue the base at the back and stick a small petal over it. Now glue in front of the small petal and stick a large one on. Repeat this until all the petals are stuck on. The curled edges of the petals should face inwards. The larger petals are placed inside, the smaller ones outside.

5. Glue the two edges at the base of the petals together so that one edge overlaps the other. Glue the thick section on the stem under the stamens; pass the stem through the petals and stick them on. Stick the calyx on and tidy the lower edge with stem tape.

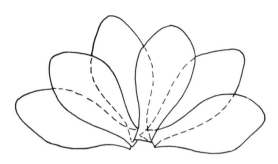

Assembling the flower

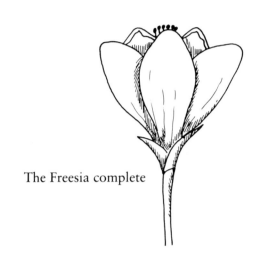

The Freesia complete

4. Cover stem wire (no. 22) with half-width stem tape. Bind the six stamens with cotton thread 13 mm ($\frac{1}{2}$ in) down the stem (half-way through, bend the tip of the stem over to secure the stamens, then complete the binding). Wrap a tiny piece of cotton wool around and over the cotton thread and cover it with stem tape.

Assembling the stamens

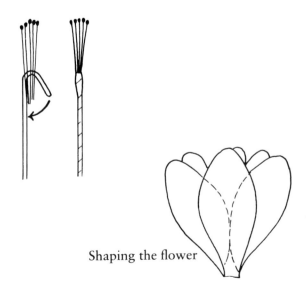

Shaping the flower

(For one flower and one leaf)

Petals
Cream polyester

Stamens
6 yellow stamens, 38 mm (1½ in) length
Cotton thread

Pistil
1 large-headed yellow stamen, 51 mm
(2 m) length

Sepals
Pink cotton

Leaf
Green cotton
1 wire (no. 26), 51 mm (2 in) length

Stem
1 wire (no. 22), 31 cm (12 in) length
Brown and green stem tape
Cotton wool

Tools required
Spade marker; 13 mm (½ in) ball goffer

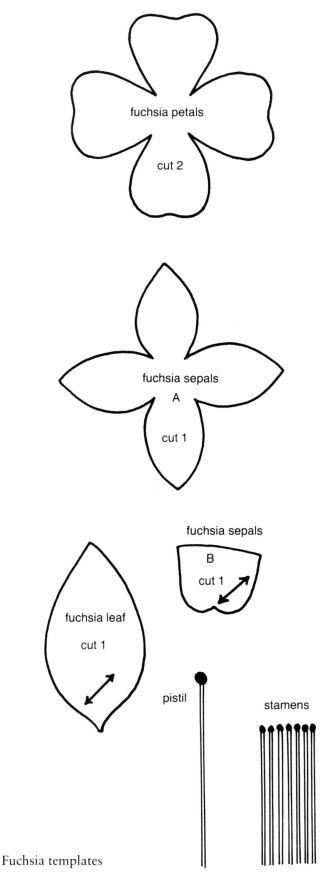

Fuchsia templates

1. Cut two sets of petals (four petals in each set) from cream polyester. Cut one set of sepals (A) and one set of sepals (B) from pink cotton. Cut one leaf from green cotton.

2. Moisten the petals and place on the 13 mm (½ in) foam rubber. Make a hollow in the petals using the ball goffer, pressing and pulling from the tip to the centre. Moisten the centre of the petals and place on the 51 mm (2 in) foam rubber. Now make a deep hollow in the centre of the petals, creating a bell shape.

3. Moisten sepals (A) and place on the 13 mm (½ in) foam rubber. Using the spade marker, make some veins on the sepals. Moisten sepals (B) and place on the 13 mm (½ in) foam rubber, then make a hollow with the ball goffer, working the tool from side to side. Make a slit in the centres of sepals (A) and the petals to allow the stem to pass through. Make veins on the leaf. Cover the 51 mm (2 in) wire (no. 26) with half-width brown stem tape and glue it on at the back of the leaf 13 mm ($\frac{1}{2}$ in) from the tip.

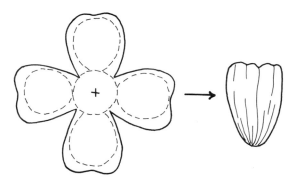

Make a bell shape from the petals

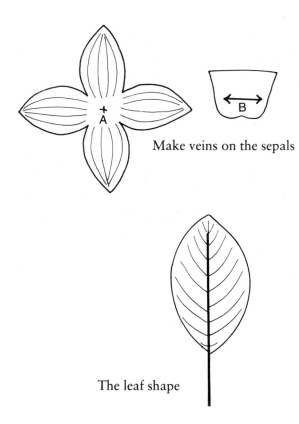

Make veins on the sepals

The leaf shape

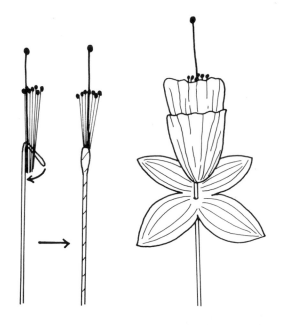

Assembling the stamens   Assembling the flower

5. Glue the thick section of the stem and pass it through one set of petals. Repeat this with the next set of petals setting them alternately. Glue on sepals (A). Now wrap a small piece of cotton wool not more than 13 mm ($\frac{1}{2}$ in) in depth around the stem under the sepals (A), making sure sepals (B) can go around it before covering it with green stem tape. Glue sepals (B) and stick it around the covered cotton wool, covering it completely. Wrap a tiny piece of cotton wool not more than 6 mm ($\frac{1}{4}$ in) in depth around the stem under sepals (B) and cover this with green stem tape. Bend the stem to tilt the flower, and attach a leaf below it.

The Fuchsia complete

4. Cover the stem wire (no. 22) with brown stem tape. Bind the six stamens and pistil with cotton thread 13 mm ($\frac{1}{2}$ in) down the stem. Half-way through, bend the tip of the stem over to secure the stamens and then complete the binding. The height of the stamens should be 25 mm (1 in) and of the pistil 38 mm ($1\frac{1}{2}$ in). Wrap a small piece of cotton wool around the bound cotton thread and cover with green stem tape.

Gypsophila

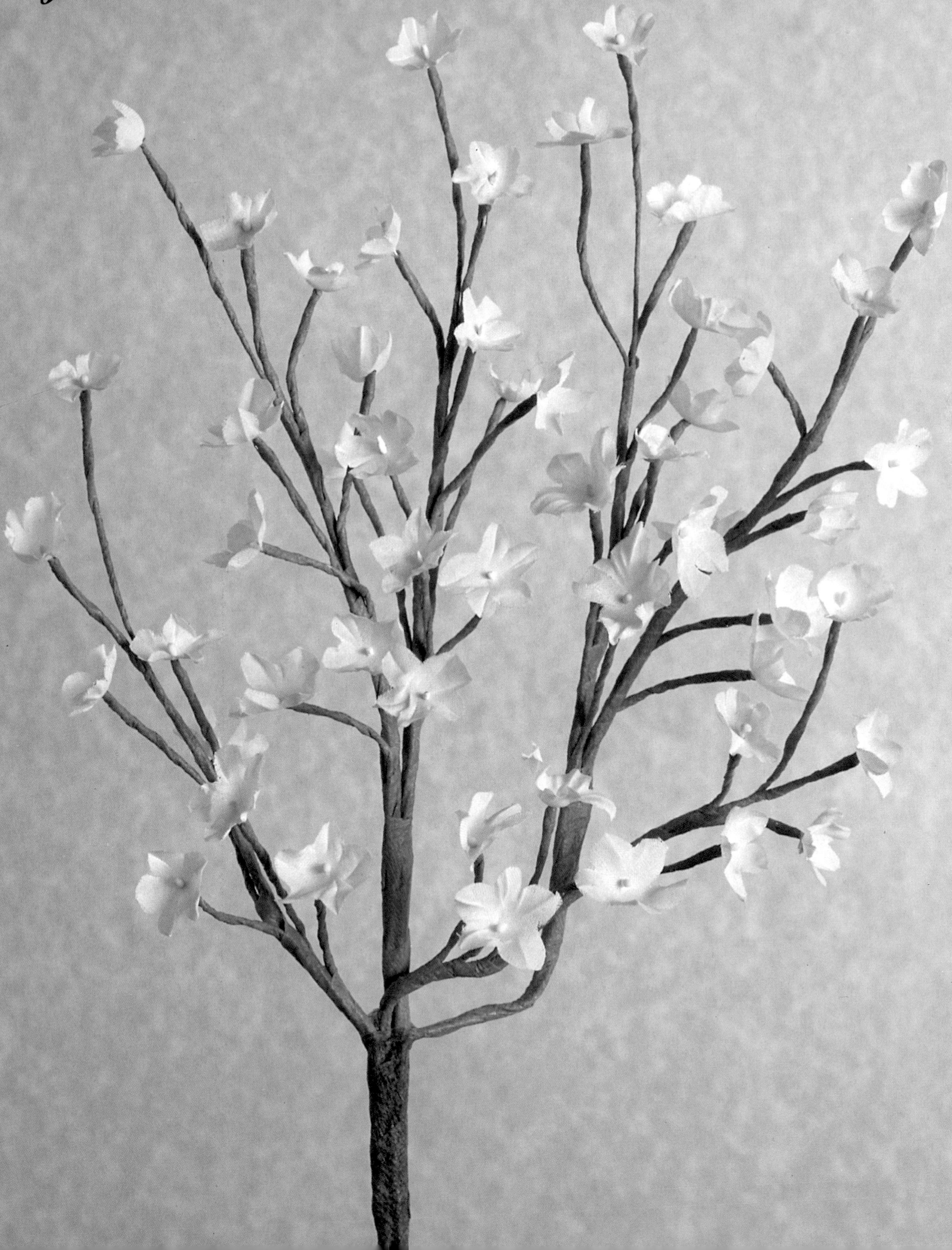

(*For ten flowers*)

Flowers
White habutai silk or cotton

Stamens
10 white or yellow stamens, 38 mm
(1½ in) lengths

Stems
10 thin wires (no. 26), 51 mm (2 in)
lengths
1 medium wire (no. 22), 30 cm (12 in)
lengths
White or pale green stem tape
(half-width)

Fabric paints
White

Tools required
Spade marker; 6 mm (¼ in) ball goffer

Gypsophila templates

large
Gypsophila

small
Gypsophila

5. Cut the 30 cm (12 in) wire into two pieces and attach the flowers in staggered positions. Now join the two main stems together with stem tape.

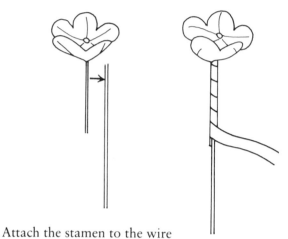

Attach the stamen to the wire

1. Cut ten flowers from the pattern. Dye with white fabric paint (if using white silk) and allow to dry. (These flowers can be cut from scraps.)

2. Moisten flowers slightly on a damp cloth and place on the 13 mm (½ in) foam rubber. Make one light vein on each petal with the spade marker and make a hollow in the centre using the ball goffer.

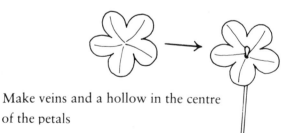

Make veins and a hollow in the centre
of the petals

3. Pierce a hole in the centre of the flower with a large needle. Thread one stamen through each flower.

4. Attach the stamen to the 51 mm (2 in) wire, winding the stem tape all the way down using a spiral motion.

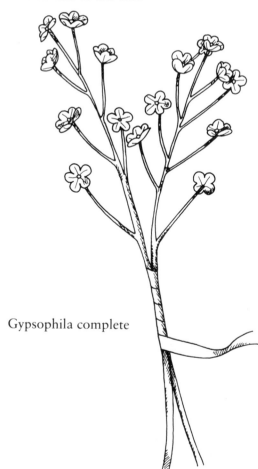

Gypsophila complete

(For three leaves)

Leaves
White thin cotton
3 thin wires (no. 26), 51 mm (2 in)
lengths
Green stem tape

Stem
1 medium wire (no. 22), 152 mm (6 in)
length
Brown stem tape

Dyes
Leaf-green

Tools required
Spade marker

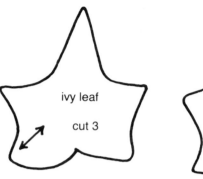
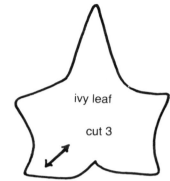

Ivy leaf templates

centre at the back of each leaf 13 mm ($\frac{1}{2}$ in) away
from the tip, extending 38 mm ($1\frac{1}{2}$ in) below the
base of the leaves.

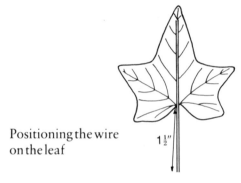

Positioning the wire
on the leaf $1\frac{1}{2}''$

4. Cover the stem wire (no. 22) with half-width
brown stem tape. Attach the leaves in alternating
positions.

1. Cut three leaves from white cotton and dye in
concentrated leaf-green dye. For a variegated ivy, use
a brush to apply dye to the leaves, missing a few
areas so that the white cotton shows through. Look
at some different types of ivy and copy their
colourings: they can be white/green, pink/green,
yellow/green or just plain green. If you want to make
the yellow/green or pink/green varieties, after
brushing on the green dye use a clean brush to apply
yellow or pink dye to the uncovered white areas.
Allow to dry.

2. Moisten leaves and place on the 13 mm ($\frac{1}{2}$ in)
foam rubber. Make veins on the leaves.

Make veins on the leaf

The Ivy leaves complete

3. Cover the three thin wires (no. 26) with
half-width green stem tape. Glue the wires in the

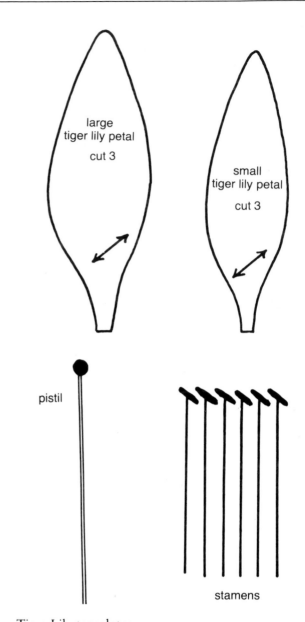

(For one flower)

Petals
Yellow satin-faced polyester or cotton fabric
6 thin wires (no. 26), 10 cm (4 in) lengths
Maroon and lime-green felt-tip pens
Light green stem tape

Stamens
6 thin wires (no. 26), 51 mm (2 in) lengths
Light green stem tape
Maroon felt-tip pen
White stem tape

Pistil
1 thin wire (no. 26), 64 mm (2½ in) length
White stem tape

Stem
1 coarse wire (no. 19), 31 cm (12 in) length
Green stem tape

Tools required
Spade marker; 13 mm (½ in) ball goffer

large tiger lily petal cut 3

small tiger lily petal cut 3

pistil

stamens

Tiger Lily templates

1. Cut three large and three small petals. Moisten the petals and place them on the 13 mm (½ in) foam rubber. Make a central vein by pressing and pulling the spade marker from the tip to the base of each petal. Turn it over using the ball goffer, then press and pull the ball goffer from the tip to the base of the petals on both sides of the central vein.

2. Cover the six thin wires (no. 26) with half-width light green stem tape and glue these at the back of the petals over the central vein, 13 mm (½ in) away from the tip, extending 13 mm (½ in) below the base. Add a very light shading with the lime-green felt-tip pen and some spots with the maroon felt-tip pen, making these denser nearer the base.

3. Cover the thin wires (no. 26) with light green stem tape. Cut a piece of full width white stem tape 13 mm (½ in) long, and wrap it firmly around one

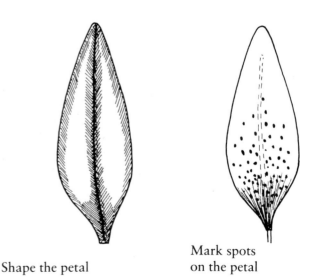

Shape the petal

Mark spots on the petal

end of the stamens wire. Now use the maroon felt-tip pen to colour in the tip and bend it into shape. Repeat for all six stamens. Make a round shape for the pistil and colour it with the maroon felt-tip pen.

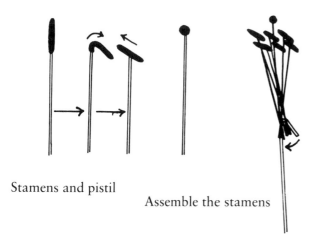

Stamens and pistil

Assemble the stamens

4. Cover the stem wire (no. 19) with green stem tape. Bind the pistil with the stamens surrounding it, using cotton thread, 13 mm ($\frac{1}{2}$ in) down the stem. Half-way through, bend the tip of the stem over to secure both stamens and pistil. Complete the binding. The height of the stamens should be 38 mm ($1\frac{1}{2}$ in), the pistil 51 mm (2 in). Cover the bound cotton with green stem tape.

5. Bind the larger petals to the stem with cotton thread, spacing them evenly where the stamens meet the stem. The remaining three petals are placed alternately. Cover the stem under the petals with green tape and bend the flower petals to shape.

The Tiger Lily complete

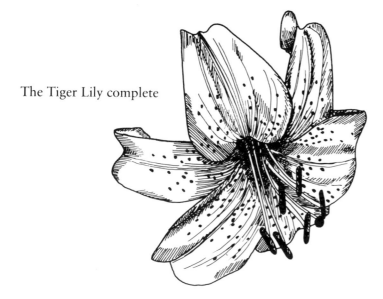

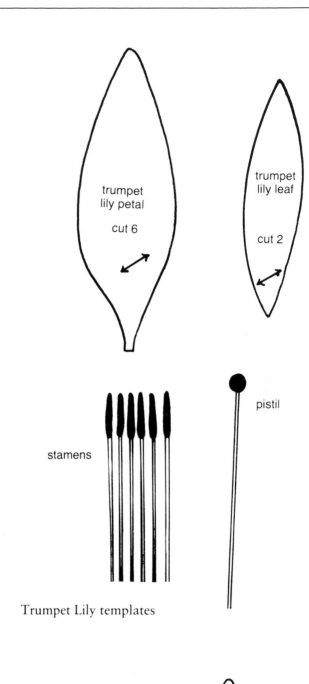

(*For one flower and two leaves*).

Petals
White satin-faced polyester or thick
cotton
6 thin wires (no. 26), 10 cm (4 in)
lengths
Light green stem tape

Stamens
6 thin wires (no. 26), 51 mm (2 in)
lengths
Cotton wool
PVA multiglue
Cotton thread
Light green stem tape

Pistil
1 thin wire (no. 26), 64 mm (2½ in)
length
Cotton wool

Stem
1 coarse wire (no. 19), 31 cm (12 in)
length
Green stem tape

Leaves
Green cotton or polyester
2 thin wires (no. 26), 64 mm (2½ in)
lengths

Dyes and fabric paint
Yellow fabric paint
Mandarin dye
Leaf-green dye

Tools required
Spade marker; 13 mm (½ in) ball goffer

trumpet
lily petal

cut 6

trumpet
lily leaf

cut 2

stamens

pistil

Trumpet Lily templates

1. Cut six petals from the white fabric and two
leaves from the green fabric. Mix a tiny amount of
yellow fabric paint with a little leaf-green dye and
add water to make a lime-green colour for the base
of the petals. Moisten the petals with a piece of
cotton wool dipped in detergent water. Now brush
the lime-green dye on the base of each petal and
allow to dry.

Brush lime-green colour on the
base of the petal

2. Moisten the petals and place on the 13 mm (½ in) foam rubber. Make a central vein by pressing and pulling the spade marker from the tip to the base of the petals. Turn the petals over, and press and pull the ball goffer from the tip to the base on both sides of the central vein. Repeat on all six petals. Cover the six 10 cm (4 in) thin wires (no. 26) with half-width light green stem tape. Stick these along the central vein at the back of the petals 13 mm (½ in) away from the tip, extending 13 mm (½ in) below the base.

3. Moisten the leaves and place them on the 13 mm (½ in) foam rubber. Make vertical veins with the spade marker. Cover the two thin wires (no. 26) with half-width green stem tape and glue them at the back of leaves 13 mm (½ in) away from the tip, extending 13 mm (½ in) below the base.

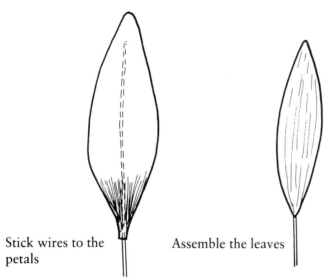

Stick wires to the petals

Assemble the leaves

4. Cover the six thin wires (no. 26) for the stamens with half-width light green stem tape and repeat with the 64 mm (2½ in) thin wire for the pistil. Thin out a piece of cotton wool by separating it into layers. Cut little strips of cotton wool about 6 mm (¼ in) × 13 mm (½ in) and wrap them around one end of the covered wire about 13 mm (½ in) deep to make the stamens. The pistil is made into a round shape. Mix a little PVA multiglue with a small amount of yellow fabric paint and a few drops of mandarin dye and water to make an orange colour. Apply this mixture to the stamens and pistil using a small brush, and leave to dry. The stamens and pistil have to be flattened with a small hammer or a metal knife handle.

5. Cover the stem wire (no. 19) with green stem tape. Bind the stamens and pistil to the stem with cotton thread 13 mm (½ in) down the stem. Bend the tip of the stem wire over before completing binding to secure stamens to stem. The height of the stamens should be 38 mm (1½ in), the pistil 51 mm (2 in). Cover the bound cotton thread with stem tape.

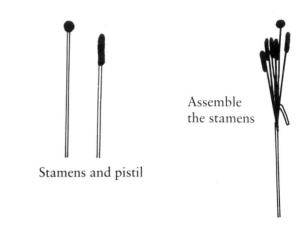

Stamens and pistil

Assemble the stamens

6. Bind three of the petals around the stamens where they meet the stem, and place the remaining three petals alternately. Cover the stem under the petals with green stem tape and attach the two leaves opposite each other.

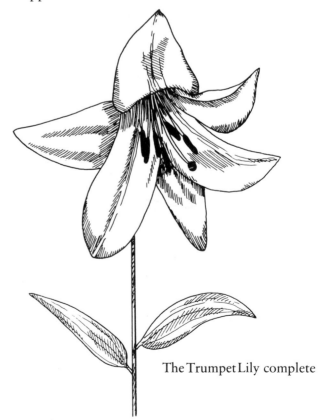

The Trumpet Lily complete

Japanese Maple

(*For three leaves*)

Leaves
Rust-red cotton or polyester lining fabric
12 thin wires (no. 26), 76 mm (3 in) lengths
3 medium wires (no. 22), 10 cm (4 in) lengths
Brown stem tape

Stem
1 coarse wire (no. 19), 20 cm (8 in) length

Tools required
Spade marker

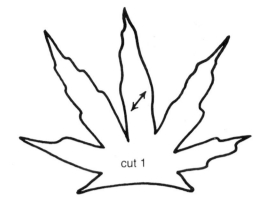

cut 1

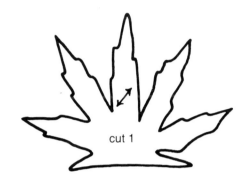

cut 1

1. Cut one large, one medium and one small leaf.

2. Moisten leaves and place on the 13 mm ($\frac{1}{2}$ in) foam rubber. Make vertical veins on the leaves with the spade marker.

3. Cover the twelve thin wires (no. 26) with half-width brown stem tape. These are the secondary support wires for the leaves. Glue them at the back of the leaves, 12 mm ($\frac{1}{2}$ in) away from the tip.

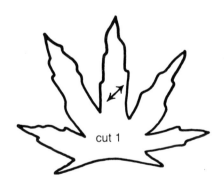

cut 1

Japanese Maple leaf templates

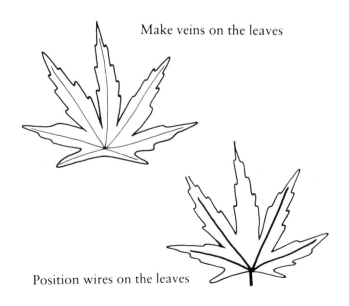

Make veins on the leaves

Position wires on the leaves

4. Cover the three medium wires (no. 22), which are the primary support wires for the leaves, with half-width brown stem tape. Glue them in the centre at the back of each leaf, 13 mm ($\frac{1}{2}$ in) away from the tip, extending 38 mm ($1\frac{1}{2}$ in) below the base. Cover the wire under the leaf with stem tape.

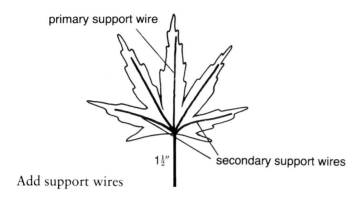

primary support wire

secondary support wires

1½″

Add support wires

5. Cover the 20 cm (8 in) stem wire with brown stem tape and attach the leaves in staggered positions with stem tape. The leaves can also be made from green fabric tinted around the edges with red fabric dye.

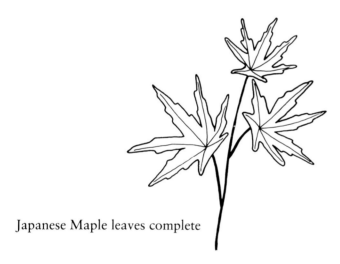

Japanese Maple leaves complete

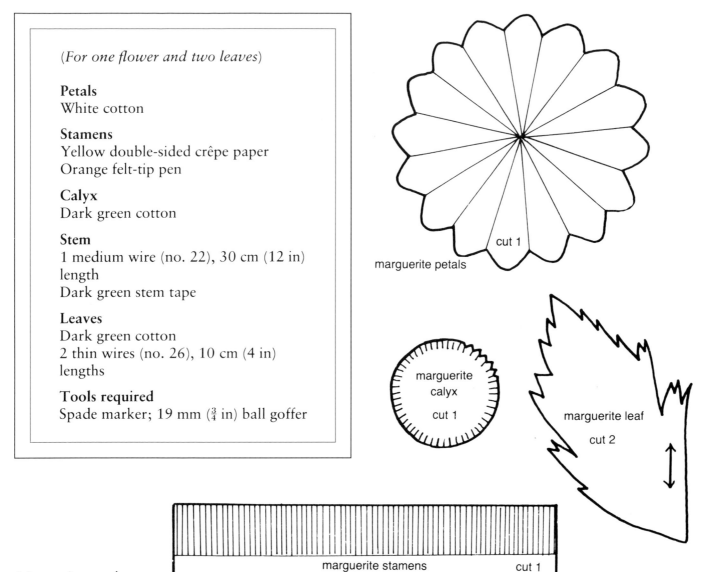

(For one flower and two leaves)

Petals
White cotton

Stamens
Yellow double-sided crêpe paper
Orange felt-tip pen

Calyx
Dark green cotton

Stem
1 medium wire (no. 22), 30 cm (12 in)
length
Dark green stem tape

Leaves
Dark green cotton
2 thin wires (no. 26), 10 cm (4 in)
lengths

Tools required
Spade marker; 19 mm (¾ in) ball goffer

cut 1

marguerite petals

marguerite
calyx

cut 1

marguerite leaf

cut 2

marguerite stamens   cut 1

Marguerite templates

1. Cut one set of petals from the white cotton, and one calyx and two leaves from the green cotton. Cut one strip of double-sided crêpe paper measuring 10 cm (4 in) × 25 mm (1 in).

2. Draw a line on both sides on one edge of the strip of stamens with the orange felt-tip pen. Make 13

mm (½ in) slits in the strip and curl the fringe using the blade of the scissors. Cover the stem wire (no. 22) with stem tape. Hook it over one end of the strip of stamens, then glue the lower edge of this and roll it evenly around the stem wire, allowing the curled fringe to fall outwards.

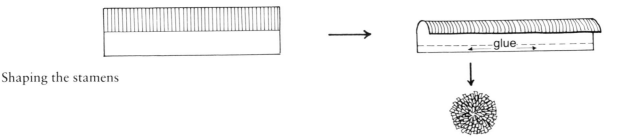

glue

Shaping the stamens

Cut and shape the petals

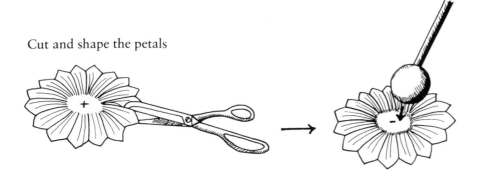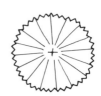

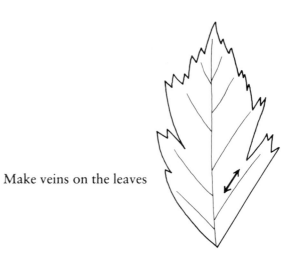

Cut a slit in the centre of the calyx

3. Moisten the set of petals and place on the 13 mm (½ in) foam rubber. Make veins on top of and in between the petals using the spade marker. Use a sharp pair of scissors to cut between and separate the petals to about 13 mm (½ in) from the centre of the piece. Now moisten the centre, turn the piece over and make a medium-depth hollow with the ball goffer. Trim off any pointed ends that are between the separated petals. Make a small slit in the centre area for the stem wire to pass through.

4. Moisten the calyx and place on the 13 mm (½ in) foam rubber. Use the spade marker to make veins all around the calyx by working the tool from the edge to the centre. Make a slit in the centre of the calyx.

5. Moisten the leaves and place on the 13 mm (½ in) foam rubber. Make the veins using the spade marker. Cover the thin wires (no. 26) with half-width stem tape and glue these in the centre at the back of the leaves 13 mm (½ in) away from the tip.

Make veins on the leaves

6. To assemble the flower, pass the stem through the slit in the set of petals. Glue under the stamens and stick them to set of petals. With all the petals facing upwards, give them a gentle squeeze so that they stick firmly to the stamens. Glue the edges of the calyx and stick it under the petals. Tidy the stem under the calyx with stem tape and finally attach the two leaves, with one slightly below the other.

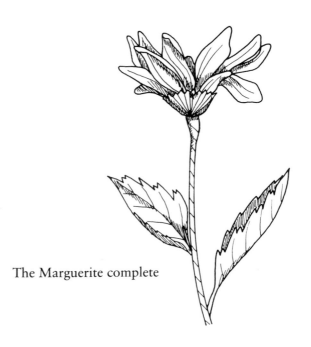

The Marguerite complete

(For one flower and three leaves)

Petals
Thin cream-coloured cotton

Corona
Thin orange cotton

Stamens
5 thin wires (no. 26), 38 mm (1½ in)
length
White stem tape
Cotton thread

Bract
White habutai silk

Stem
1 coarse wire (no. 19), 31 cm (12 in)
length
1 plastic tube 4 mm (⅛ in) diameter, 28
cm (11 in) length
Green stem tape

Leaves
Thick green cotton
3 medium wires (no. 22), 20 cm (8 in)
lengths

Dyes and fabric paint
Mandarin and leaf green dyes
Yellow fabric paint

Tools required
Spade marker; 19 mm (¾ in) ball goffer;
chaser goffer

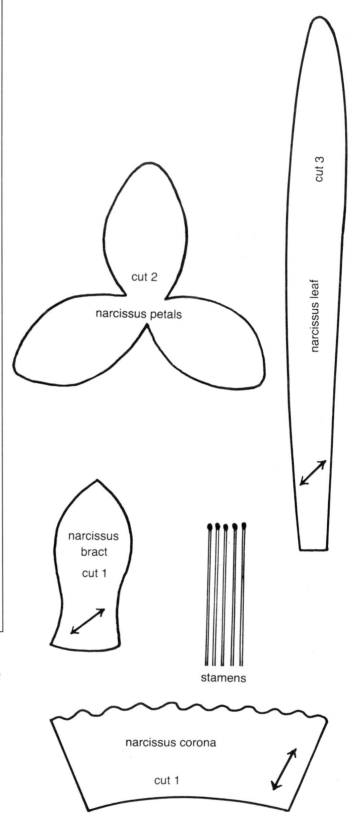

cut 2

narcissus petals

cut 3

narcissus leaf

narcissus
bract

cut 1

stamens

narcissus corona

cut 1

Narcissus templates

1. Cut two sets of petals from the cream cotton, one bract from the white habutai silk and three leaves from the green cotton. Cut one corona from the orange cotton. Mix a little mandarin and leaf-green dye with water to make a light brown colour, and use it to dye the bract.

2. Moisten the petals and place them on the 13 mm (½ in) foam rubber or a tea-towel folded into four to make a hard surface. Make vertical veins with the spade marker, working the tool from the top to the base of the petals. Moisten the centre of the set of

petals; place it on the 13 mm (½ in) foam rubber and use the ball goffer to make a slight hollow in the centre.

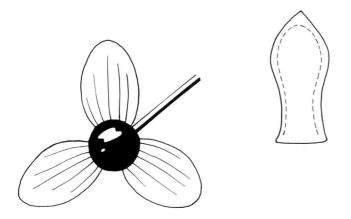

Shape the petals and bract

3. Moisten the bract and place it on the 13 mm (½ in) foam rubber. Press and pull the ball goffer from the top to the base. Moisten the leaves and make vertical veins on each leaf, pressing the spade marker very lightly. Cover the three medium wires (no. 22) with green stem tape and glue these at the back of each leaf, 13 mm (½ in) away from the tip.

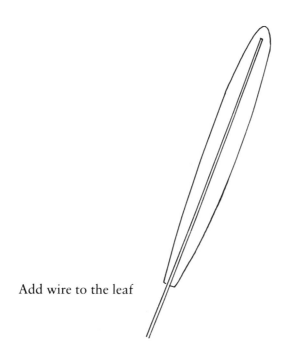

Add wire to the leaf

4. Moisten the corona and place it on the 13 mm (½ in) foam rubber. Make creases with the chaser goffer by pressing and pulling it from each curved point to the base of the corona. Make a running stitch about 6 mm (¼ in) from the base, leaving a piece of excess cotton to bind the corona to the stem.

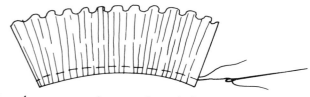

Gather the corona using running stitch

5. Cover about 51 mm (2 in) of stem wire with green stem tape. Now cover the five thin wires (no. 26) with half-width white stem tape to make the stamens. Make the head (anthers) of the stamens by winding another small piece of half-width white stem tape on one end of each stamen, keeping it to a depth of not more than 6 mm (¼ in). Mix a little yellow fabric paint with water and apply it all over each of the stamens. Use a small brush to apply a small spot of yellow fabric paint to the head of each stamen to make it stand out. Allow to dry.

6. Bind the five stamens about 13 mm (½ in) down the covered end of the stem wire. Half-way through, bend the tip of the stem over, then complete the binding. Glue the edges of the corona to make a tube. Pull the cotton thread of the running stitches so that it forms an even gather, then pass the stem wire through the corona, position it where the stamens meet the stem, and bind the corona to the stem with the excess cotton thread. Cover the bound cotton thread with stem tape. Glue the stem under the corona and pass the stem through the plastic tube and stick.

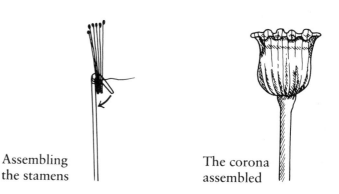

Assembling the stamens

The corona assembled

7. Make a slit in the centre of both sets of petals.
Glue under the corona about 13 mm ($\frac{1}{2}$ in) from the
stem, then pass the stem through one set of petals
and stick it to the corona. Glue under these petals
and stick the second set of petals on, arranging them
to lie in the gaps in the first set. Cover the stem
completely with green stem tape. Glue the base of
the bract and stick it about 38 mm ($1\frac{1}{2}$ in) down the
stem below the flower. Bend the stem over slightly so
that the flower tilts.

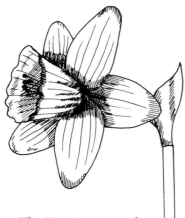

The Narcissus complete

(*For one flower and two leaves*)

Petals
White habutai silk

Calyx
Green cotton

Stem
1 medium wire (no. 22), 20 cm (8 in) length
Green stem tape

Leaves
Green cotton
2 thin wires (no. 26), 76 mm (3 in) length

Dyes
Camellia

Tools required
Chaser goffer; 13 mm (½ in) ball goffer; spade marker

large pink petals
cut 3

small pink petals
cut 3

pink leaf
cut 2

calyx
cut 1

Pink templates

1. Cut three large and three small sets of petals (six petals in each set) from white silk, and one calyx and two leaves from green cotton. Dye petals to the required shade of pink by mixing camellia dye with water (a different shade of dye can be used to tint the edges of the petals using a fine brush). Allow to dry.

2. Moisten the small petals and place on the 13 mm (½ in) foam rubber. Make creases using the chaser goffer. Press and pull the tool from the tip to the centre of the petals, releasing pressure as you pull. Moisten the centre of the petals and place on the 51 mm (2 in) foam rubber. Make a deep hollow with the 13 mm (½ in) ball goffer by pressing the tool in the centre of the petals. Moisten the larger petals, place on the 13 mm (½ in) foam rubber and make creases using the chaser goffer. Moisten the centre of the petals, turn them over and make a light hollow. Moisten the leaves and place on the 13 mm (½ in) foam rubber. Using the pointed tip of the spade marker, press and pull from the tip to the base. Cover the two thin wires (no. 26) with half-width stem tape, and glue these in the centre at the back of the leaves 13 mm (½ in) away from the tip.

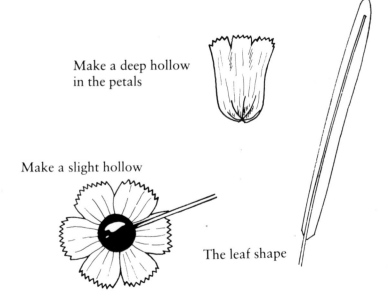

Make a deep hollow in the petals

Make a slight hollow

The leaf shape

3. Cover the stem wire (no. 22) with stem tape. Wrap a small piece of cotton wool (the size of a pea) around one end of the stem. Half-way, bend the tip of the stem over to secure the cotton wool. Cover with stem tape. Make a small slit in the centre of all the petals. Glue the tip and base of the cotton bud, then pass the stem through one of the smaller sets of petals and stick them closely to the cotton bud. Now glue half-way up and around the base, and stick the second set on. Repeat this for the third set. Glue underneath the small petals and stick on the larger sets of petals, setting them alternately.

4. Wrap a small piece of cotton wool around the stem under the petals to make the base for the calyx. Make sure the calyx fits around the base before covering the cotton wool with stem tape. Glue and stick on the calyx. Tidy the join between the calyx and stem using stem tape. Attach the leaves opposite each other with stem tape.

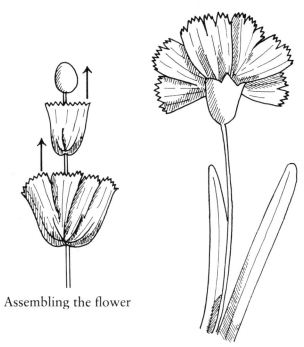

Assembling the flower

The Pink complete

Poinsettia

84

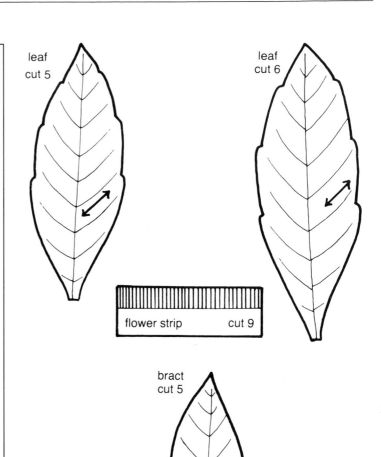

leaf
cut 5

leaf
cut 6

flower strip   cut 9

bract
cut 5

Poinsettia templates

(For *nine flowers, five bracts and eleven leaves*)

Flowers
Yellow double-sided crêpe paper
Cotton wool
9 thin wires (no. 26), 38 mm (1½ in)
lengths
Green stem tape
Cotton thread

Bracts
Red polyester (lining) fabric or thin
cotton
5 thin wires (no. 26), 64 mm (2½ in)
lengths
Green stem tape

Leaves
Same fabric as bracts
5 thin wires (no. 26), 76 mm (3 in)
lengths
6 thin wires (no. 26), 89 mm (3½ in)
lengths
Green stem tape

Stem
1 coarse wire (no. 19), 20 cm (8 in)
length
Green stem tape

Tools required
Spade marker

1. Cut nine strips of yellow double-sided crêpe paper 38 mm (1½ in) × 13 mm (½ in). Cut five bracts, five small leaves and six large leaves. Moisten the bracts and place them on the 13 mm (½ in) foam rubber. Make veins with the spade marker. Moisten the leaves and make veins in the same way as on the bracts. Cover the thin wires (no. 26) for the bracts and both large and small leaves with half-width stem tape. Glue these in the centre at the back of the bracts and leaves 13 mm (½ in) away from the tip extending 13 mm (½ in) below the base. Use the 64 mm (2½ in) wires for the bracts, the 76 mm (3 in) for the smaller leaves and the 89 mm (3½ in) for the larger leaves.

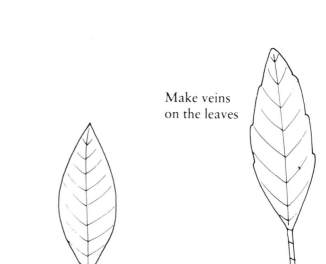

Make veins
on the leaves

Make veins on the bracts

2. For the flowers, make 6 mm (¼ in) slits on the strips of double-sided crêpe paper. Curve the fringe with the blade of the scissors. Cover the nine 38 mm (1½ in) thin wires (no. 26) with half-width stem tape. Wrap a small piece of cotton wool the size of a small pea around one end of the covered wire (half-way through, bend the tip of the wire over to secure the cotton wool). Now glue the lower edge of the strip of double-sided crêpe paper and roll it evenly around the cotton wool bud allowing the fringe to fall inwards. Cover half of the fringe with half-width stem tape. Repeat this for all nine flowers.

3. Cover the stem wire (no. 19) with the stem tape. Bind all the flowers around the stem with cotton thread; half-way through binding, bend the tip of the stem over, then complete. The flowers should be 25 mm (1 in) in height from the stem. Add the bracts, spacing them evenly around the flowers, and bind them with cotton thread. Add the smaller leaves, followed by the larger ones, arranging them alternately. Cut off the ends of cotton thread and cover the bound thread with stem tape.

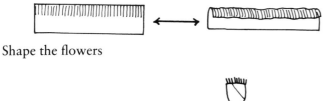

Shape the flowers

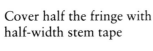

Cover half the fringe with half-width stem tape

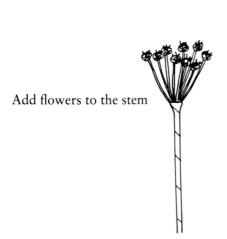

Add flowers to the stem

The Poinsettia complete

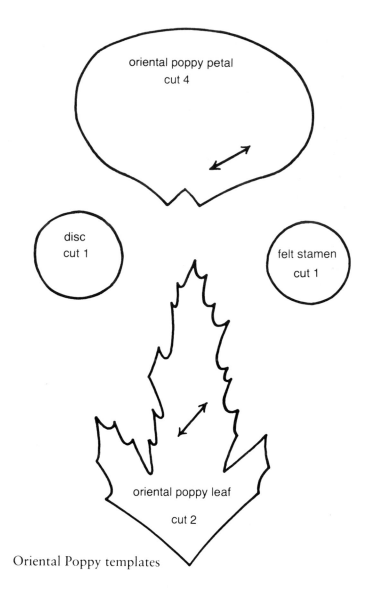

Oriental Poppy templates

(For one flower and two leaves)

Petals
Red thin cotton
Dark brown stem tape
Black felt-tip pen
4 thin wires (no. 26), 51 mm (2 in)
lengths

Stamens
Black felt fabric
Cotton wool

Disc
Pale green thin cotton
Cotton thread

Stem
1 medium wire (no. 22), 30 cm (12 in)
length
Green stem tape

Leaves
Green cotton
2 thin wires (no. 26), 10 cm (4 in)
lengths

Tools required
Curler goffer; spade marker

1. Cut four petals from the red cotton, one disc from the pale green cotton, two leaves from the green cotton and one stamen from black felt fabric. Make a running stitch around the edge of the disc, leaving a piece of cotton thread at the end to bind the disc to the stem. Cover the stem wire (no. 22) with stem tape and wrap a small piece of cotton wool the size of a pea around one end. Bend the tip of the wire over to secure the cotton wool before you mould it to a ball. Place the disc over the cotton ball and pull the cotton thread tightly around the stem, binding it with the excess cotton thread. Make 6 mm ($\frac{1}{4}$ in) slits around the edge of the stamens to make a fringe and slit in the centre. Glue under the disc, pass the stem through stamens and stick it.

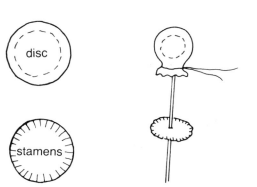

Assembling the stamens

2. Moisten the petals and place on the 13 mm (½ in) foam rubber. Make a fluted edge on the petals using the curler goffer to press and pull five times on each petal, starting in the centre tip. Cover the thin wires (no. 26) with half-width brown stem tape and glue these in the centre at the back of each petal, leaving 13 mm (½ in) from the tip extending 19 mm (¾ in) below the base of the petals. Glue and stick one point so that it overlaps the other at the base at the back of the petals. Use the black felt-tip pen to mark the base of the petals. Moisten the leaves and make veins with the spade marker. Cover the two thin wires (no. 26) with half-width green stem tape, then glue these in the centre at the back of the leaves, 13 mm (½ in) away from the tip.

3. Bind two petals opposite each other with cotton thread. Fill in the gaps with the two remaining petals. Cover the bound cotton and petal wires with green stem tape. Attach the leaves one below the other on opposite sides, using stem tape.

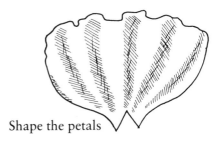

Shape the petals

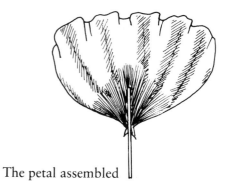

The petal assembled

The Oriental Poppy complete

(For one flower, one bud and six leaves)

Petals
White habutai silk

Bud petals
White habutai silk
Cotton wool
Cotton thread

Calyxes
Green cotton

Leaves
Green cotton
4 thin wires (no. 26), 51 mm (2 in) length
2 thin wires (no. 26), 10 cm (4 in) length
Green stem tape

Stems
2 coarse wires (no. 19), 31 cm (12 in) length
Green stem tape

Dyes
Yellow

Tools required
Curler goffer; spade marker; 19 mm ($\frac{3}{4}$ in) ball goffer

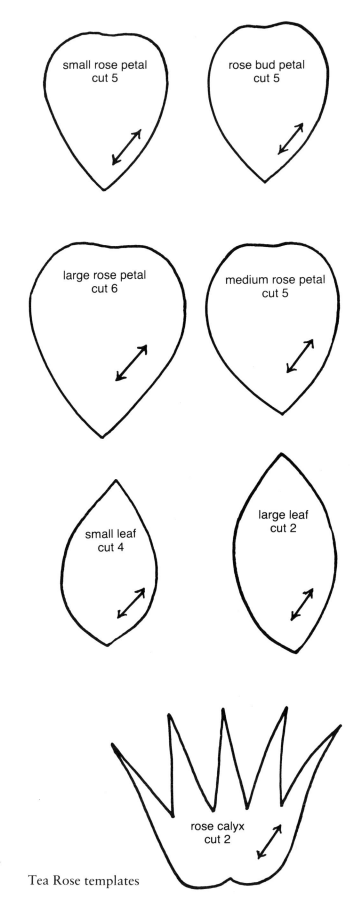

small rose petal
cut 5

rose bud petal
cut 5

large rose petal
cut 6

medium rose petal
cut 5

small leaf
cut 4

large leaf
cut 2

rose calyx
cut 2

Tea Rose templates

1. Cut six large, five medium and five small petals for the flower and five petals for the bud, all from white silk. Cut two large leaves, four small leaves and two calyxes from green cotton.

2. Next dye the petals, mixing the dye to the colour required. First dye the five petals for the bud, then add half a teaspoon of cold water to the remaining dye to make the colour a little lighter. Dye the small flower petals, then dilute the dye again for the medium-sized petals. A further dilution is made to dye the large petals. Allow to dry.

3. Moisten the five small petals for the flowers and place them on the 13 mm ($\frac{1}{2}$ in) foam rubber. Slightly curl the edges of the petals with the spade marker.

91

Moisten the base and the centre of the petals, and place them on the 51 cm (2 in) foam rubber. Press and pull from the centre to the base of the petals with the ball goffer, making a deep hollow at the base. Repeat, using the same shaping, for the bud petals.

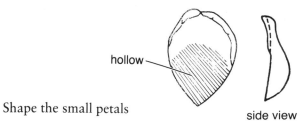

Shape the small petals

side view

4. Moisten the five medium petals and place on the 13 mm (½ in) foam rubber. Curl the edges with the spade marker. Moisten the centre and the base of the petals, turn them over and place on the 51 mm (2 in) foam rubber. Make a hollow in the centre of the petals by pressing lightly with the ball goffer, working the tool from side to side. Now press the ball goffer down as far as it will go to make a deep hollow on the base of the petals.

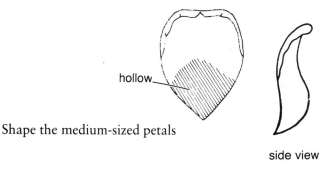

hollow

Shape the medium-sized petals

side view

5. Moisten the edges of the larger petals and place them on the 13 mm (½ in) foam rubber. Using the pointed tip of the spade marker, press and make a very short pull around the edges. Make a slightly larger curl by using the curler goffer on all the large petals. Now moisten the base of the petals, turn them over and make a light hollow.

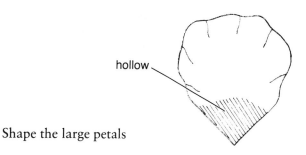

hollow

Shape the large petals

6. Moisten the leaves and make veins with the spade marker. Serrate the edges of the leaves. Cover the thin wires (no. 26) with half-width stem tape. Glue the longer wires to the centre back of the larger leaves, and the shorter wires to the smaller leaves. Join one large leaf with two small leaves with stem tape to make a set.

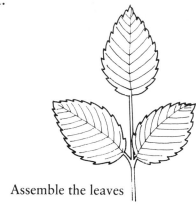

Assemble the leaves

7. Moisten the calyxes, make veins on all five points with the spade marker, turn them over and make a hollow with the ball goffer, working the tool from side to side.

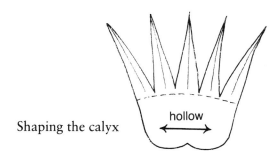

Shaping the calyx

hollow

8. Cover the stem wires (no. 19) with stem tape. Wrap a piece of cotton wool around one end of both stem wires to form the inner core for both flower and bud. Before completing, bend the tip of the stems over to secure the cotton wool. Now mould these into a bud shape.

The bud shape

9. To assemble the bud, wind some cotton thread around the stem under the bud, ready to bind the petals as you glue them to the bud. Glue one petal and stick it closely around the cotton wool bud, almost covering it. Use the cotton thread to bind the petals as you glue them on. Glue the second petal on, sticking it opposite the first petal: this should cover the cotton bud completely. Add the remaining three petals, spacing them around the bud. Wrap a piece of cotton wool around the stem of the bud to form the base for the calyx. Cover the cotton wool with stem tape and glue the calyx over it. Wrap a piece of fine wire or cotton thread around the calyx to swell it. Leave it for a minute before removing.

above to swell it. Attach one set of leaves to the rose, and the other to the bud, about 76 mm (3 in) below the calyx using stem tape.

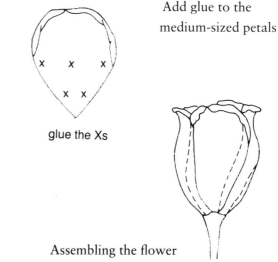

Add glue to the medium-sized petals

glue the Xs

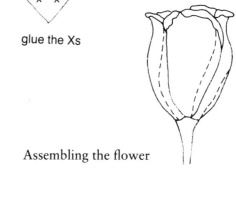

Assembling the flower

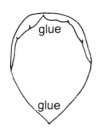

Glue the bud petals

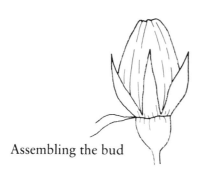

Assembling the bud

The Tea Rose complete

10. To assemble the flower, use the second prepared cotton wool bud and make up in the same way as the bud, using cotton thread to bind each petal individually. Now add the five medium-sized petals, applying glue sparingly to each. Space the petals evenly around, overlapping each other. Glue the base of the larger petals and bind them around the medium petals, again so that they overlap. Wrap a piece of cotton wool around the stem under the flower to form the base of the calyx, and cover with stem tape. Glue on the calyx, repeating the method

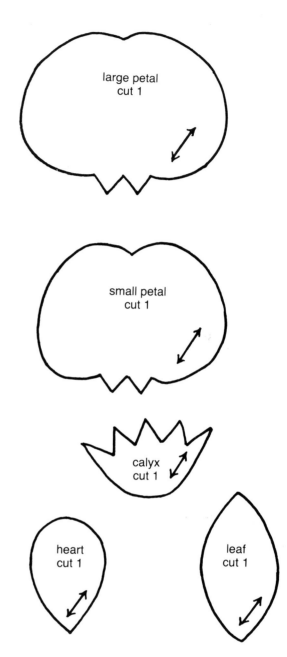

(For one flower and one leaf)

Petals
Pale yellow polyester lining fabric

Heart
Bright yellow polyester lining fabric

Calyx
Green cotton

Stem
1 thin wire (no. 26), 180 mm (7 in)
length
Green stem tape

Leaf
Green cotton
1 thin wire (no. 26), 76 mm (3 in)
length

Tools required
Curler goffer; 13 mm (½ in) ball goffer;
spade marker

large petal
cut 1

small petal
cut 1

calyx
cut 1

heart
cut 1

leaf
cut 1

Sweet Pea templates

1. Cut one large and one small petal from the pale yellow fabric, one heart from the bright yellow fabric, and one calyx and one leaf from the green cotton. Moisten the petals and place them on the 13 mm (½ in) foam rubber. Press the curler goffer on the edges of the petals and pull to half-way down to make a fluted edge on both large and small petals. Make a 13 mm (½) slit at the base of the small petal, and stick so that one point is overlapping the other at the base.

Shape the petals

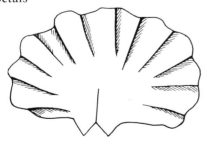

Fold the base of
the small petal

95

2. Moisten the heart and place on the 51 mm (2 in) foam rubber. Make a deep hollow using the ball goffer (press and pull from the tip to the base). Moisten the calyx and make light veins on all five points. Moisten the leaf and make veins with the spade marker. Cover the 76 mm (3 in) thin wire (no. 26) with half-width stem tape. Glue this at the back of the leaf 13 mm (½ in) away from the tip. Cover the stem wire (no. 26) with half-width stem tape. Wrap a small piece of cotton wool around one end of the stem (half-way through, bend the tip of the stem over to secure the cotton wool, which should be the size of a small pea). Now glue the edges around the heart and stick it over the cotton wool bud.

3. Glue the back of the large petal at the base and stick it to the back of the small petal at the base so that they are stuck back to back. Glue the base of the small petal and stick it to the base of the heart. Glue the calyx on and tidy the join between the calyx and the stem. Attach the leaf with stem tape about 76 mm (3 in) below the flower.

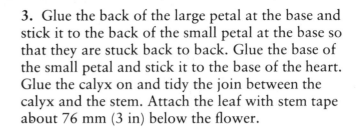

small petal

large petal

Assembling the flower

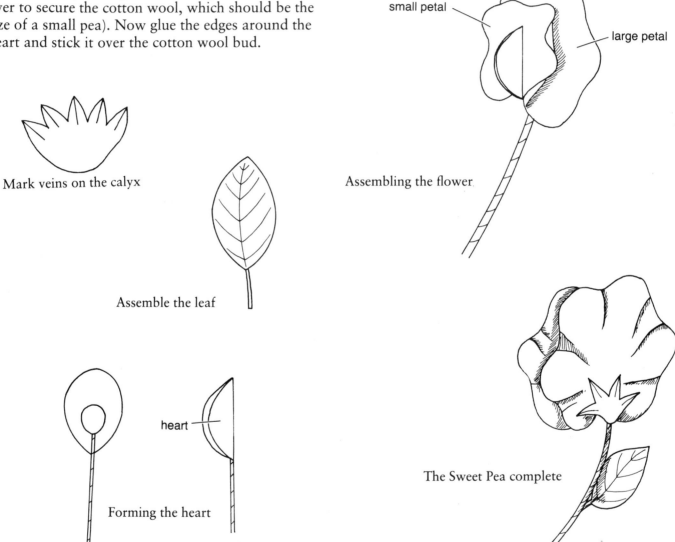

Mark veins on the calyx

Assemble the leaf

heart

Forming the heart

The Sweet Pea complete